The Illusion of Separation

Praise for *The Illusion of Separation*

Robert Sardello, PhD, author of *Love and the Soul: Creating a Future for Earth*

'Giles Hutchins takes us on an amazing tour de force, the intellectual tour of our lives. With ease and incredible clarity, he reveals simultaneously the history and the philosophy and the implications of the dire plight Earth is now within... Never before, that I know of, has the choice of life, true life, or the path of degradation been put before us with such clear equanimity.'

Catherine Keller, Professor of Constructive Theology, Drew University, author of *On the Mystery*

'Cutting through habitual denials and academic evasions, Giles Hutchins exposes the delusion at the root of our planetary crisis. And with a holographic richness of resources and disciplines, he discloses—indeed activates—the attitude that might just provoke our needed evolution. This is a wise and urgent text: may it be heard, and soon!'

Llewellyn Vaughan-Lee, PhD, Sufi teacher and author of *Spiritual Ecology: The Cry of the Earth*

'With clarity and insight Giles Hutchins analyses the roots of our present collective mindset of separation, and yet shows how science and spirituality point to a deeper, inclusive consciousness. Here are signposts for a future that is vitally needed in the present moment.'

Tim Smit, KBE, founder of The Eden Project

'This is a powerful and timely work that asks the most important question of all... Have we evolved from Homo sapiens sapiens (so good we named ourselves twice) into Homo Hubris - the ape that lost its nature.'

Chris Laszlo, PhD, author of *Flourishing Enterprise: The New Spirit of Business*

'A treasure of a book that I will share widely; a brilliantly written insightful tour de force.'

For more praise see page 202

The
Illusion of
Separation

Exploring the Cause of our Current Crises

GILES HUTCHINS

Floris Books

First published in 2014 by Floris Books
© 2014 Giles Hutchins

Illustrations by Stefanie Koehler of
BCI: Biomimicry for Creative Innovation
at www.businessinspiredbynature.com

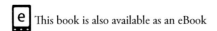 This book is also available as an eBook

British Library CIP Data available
ISBN 978-178250-127-5
Printed in Poland

This book is dedicated to Nature and her magical ways, and also to my daughter Lilly-Belle who, like all daughters and sons, is a uniquely beautiful expression of Nature.

Contents

Introduction   11

PART ONE: LIVING WITHIN THE ILLUSION

Chapter 1.   The Short Story of Consumerism   16

Chapter 2.   A Dog-Eat-Dog World   23

Chapter 3.   The Cartesian Separation   31

Chapter 4.   The Formation of Western Philosophy   38

Chapter 5.   The Fall   54

Chapter 6.   The Evolution of Western Ways of Attending   63

PART TWO: THE THINNING OF THE VEIL

Chapter 7.   Nature's Ways of Relating   75

Chapter 8.   Quantum Reality   87

Chapter 9.   Beyond Dualism   95

Chapter 10. An Awakened Way of Relating   106

Chapter 11. Awakening the Self   112

Chapter 12. The Heart and Soul of It   121

Chapter 13. Indigenous Wisdom   127

Chapter 14. Crossing the Threshold   134

PART THREE: SEEING BEYOND

Chapter 15. The Communion of Opposing Tensions   142

Chapter 16. Natural Inclusion   148

Chapter 17. The New Paradigm   158

Chapter 18. The Awakening   169

Endnotes   174

References   187

Index   195

Acknowledgments

Only those who will risk going too far can possibly find out how far one can go.

T.S. Eliot[1]

In writing this book I have pushed the envelope of my own understanding. I do not profess to be an expert in the deep areas I explore here and have gained inspiration from many sources and experts, far more learned than I, whose work is detailed in the Endnotes and References. Here I would like to explicitly acknowledge people who have directly engaged with me during the many months of developing, writing and editing this book: Iain McGilchrist, Rupert Sheldrake, Tim Smit, Simon Robinson, Chris Laszlo, Christopher Moore, Nick Bellorini, Carolyn Lebel, Stefanie Koehler, Emma Kidd, Nadine Andrews, Sue Blagburn and Mike Edwards. I would like to acknowledge particular thanks to Roy Reynolds (for his deep insights and edits on a number of sections), to Joseph Milne (for his invaluable contributions to Chapter Four), to Howard Williams (for his unwavering support), to Spencer Williams (for encouraging me to go one step beyond), to my wife Star (for living up to her name) and last, but not least, to Alan Rayner (for his advice, edits, numerous insights and companionship throughout).

Introduction

I regard the grooves of destiny into which our civilization has entered as a special case of evolutionary cul-de-sac. Courses which offered short-term advantage have been adopted, have become rigidly programmed, and have begun to prove disastrous over longer time. This is the paradigm for extinction by way of loss of flexibility.

Gregory Bateson[1]

What has become widely referred to as 'Western civilisation' has brought great technological advancement and social change over the millennia. Its underpinning scientific-philosophy is now the dominant paradigm in most parts of our world, regarded by many as the only viable way ahead and a panacea for all our ills. The cultural belief has grown that, with enough time and money, all problems can be solved through this science and technology. One has only to be reminded of the great strides we have made in, for instance, computing, manufacturing, medicine and food production to recognise the attraction of this creed.

Yet something is amiss. We seem to be facing increasingly insurmountable social, psychological, economic and environmental problems of epic proportions. Many are now recognising that these problems run deep and wide. These are pivotal times for humanity. And yet the regular reaction to our plethora of problems is to find scientific, monetary or technological fixes way downstream from the inherent problems themselves. All too often these downstream fixes actually exacerbate the underlying problems. As the scholar Joseph Milne notes, 'There is a tendency in our age to rush to change the manifest effects of wrong actions without seriously considering the root causes.'[2]

Have we become addicted to a pathway that undermines our very evolution? Are our sustainability initiatives optimising inherently unsustainable strategies? Would it not be wiser to take sufficient pause to explore and reveal the root causes of our many crises and remedy them there rather than trying in vain to deal with their ever deepening, spreading and complicating down-stream ramifications? By stepping back to ponder, we can start to identify the ensemble of intrinsic, culturally embedded problems within our social, economic, scientific and philosophical Western paradigms – for convenience referred to collectively herein as the 'Western paradigm'.

Far from our Western paradigm being the grand solution-provider to all our ills, many prominent thinkers in business, politics, education, society, the arts and sciences point to its role in actually fuelling the multiple crises. For instance, the much admired award-winning former Chairman and CEO of Interface, Ray Anderson explained, 'We have been, and still are, in the grips of a flawed view of reality – a flawed paradigm, a flawed world view – and it pervades our culture putting us on a biological collision course with collapse.'[3] Christine Lagarde, Head of the International Monetary Fund points out that 'we are currently subsidising the destruction of our planet on an enormous scale.'[4] And contemporary writer C.J. Moore notes that:

> Many of our accepted practices and beliefs have brought us, and our planet, to a place of extreme vulnerability and dire ugliness ... Governments and institutions that should have been protectors of society and landscape, have played into the hands of commerce and short term profiteering.[5]

While this Western paradigm has brought much material betterment (details of which are well versed) it has an insidious, cancerous quality causing it to undermine our very existence. Its historic tendency has been to colonise new lands and 'markets' in a way that is fundamentally destructive to its host, like cancer does. Put bluntly, our prevalent way of attending is systemically anti-life. There are ample books, research papers and scientific studies exploring in detail the damage inflicted by modern humanity upon our biosphere and it is assumed the reader is either aware of, or can find out with ease, the current demise of life on Earth which goes far deeper than the hot topic of climate change. For instance, bio-diversity loss on Earth is now assumed to be happening at a rate of somewhere between 100–1000 times faster than background rates. Another obvious warning sign is the gigantic 'plastic islands' now coalescing in our oceans. The one in the Pacific Ocean known as the 'Great Pacific Garbage Patch' is thought to be larger than the size of France and growing by the day. This systemically anti-life behaviour begs the questions, 'Are we able to change our way of living to one that is supportive of, rather than destructive to, life? If so, how and how fast?' These are pivotal questions for our time. This book takes us on a journey upstream to find root causes and then sets about exploring ways of attending to life that could overcome these corruptions. Clearly this small book cannot hope to provide definitive answers if there were such things – and indeed, as we shall explore, the quest for certainty through definitive logic is at the root of our present difficulties – yet it is hoped that the pages ahead provide an accessible exploration of:

◊   How the Western paradigm developed in the way it has done and what the root causes of this carcinogenic way of attending may be (by 'attending' is meant our overall experiencing of life – analysing, perceiving, relating, engaging, and embodying);
◊   Ways to rectify these root causes at source;
◊   A way ahead which does not constrain itself with the same thinking that caused the problems in the first place.

In Part One we start from the present day situation of consumerism which we seem so hopelessly dependent upon in the West. We explore how the Freudian desire to control the irrational aspects of our psyche influenced a perceived need to manipulate society through consumerism. Then we take a step upstream, back in time, to Darwinism and the way in which we came to view the world through the lens of competition. We explore how this perception originates with the abstraction of separating content from context and how this goes hand-in-hand with capitalism and the desire for control through socio-economic systems. From here we go further upstream to the Scientific Revolution of the sixteenth and seventeenth century. We explore how our Western mind became predominantly materialistic, whereupon Nature was perceived as a collection of objects to be controlled and manipulated. From here we venture yet further upstream in search of the formation of Western philosophy in ancient Greece. We also explore the rise of Christendom in Europe during medieval times and its effect on our way of perceiving life.

Then finally, we forge further upstream to the springs of civilisation and the invasions of Neolithic Europe in search of how domination and control came to pervade Western culture.

Having identified potential root causes and their restrictive effects, in Part Two we start to re-view life beyond these restrictions, unshackled, as it were, from ingrained cultural habituations. We start off by exploring Nature's myriad ways of relating. Then we take a brief look at the exciting discoveries of quantum physics and how our perception of space, energy and matter can deepen beyond mechanistic materialism. This leads us on into exploring some interesting Western theories about the relation of consciousness and matter. We then explore some profound developments in Western thought which point to life beyond the tidy confines of objectified science: phenomenology, process philosophy, participatory consciousness and ecological psychology. Then our own psyche and conscious awareness is explored within a journey of self-realisation. This leads us on to a deeper perspective of our imagination, heart and soul. And then, the ancient yet timeless wisdom of indigenous cultures is related to all that has been understood so far in our explorations. Finally, the concept of a 'paradigm shift' is discussed along with what leadership capabilities this may call upon. Having explored Western conceptual thinking, we can then dive into a new way of embracing life in Part Three.

Clearly this book has a wide scope and yet it has been limited to the Western way of attending not least because I have experienced it first-hand, but also because of its profound influence on the world stage today. Insights from non-Western ways of attending have played a significant role in formulating what is explored here. The hope is that varied and entwining aspects of this scope have been shared in a tractable way so that you can enjoy this exploration and feel free to pick up and put down this book between passages amidst the busyness of daily life. If you would like to further discuss experiences and insights, or read further material related to what is explored here, please visit www.thenatureofbusiness.org.

Let us commence!

Part One:

Living Within The Illusion

1. The Short Story of Consumerism[1]

Greed, envy, sloth, pride and gluttony: these are not vices anymore.
No, these are marketing tools. Lust is our way of life. Envy is just a
nudge towards another sale. Even in our relationships we consume
each other, each of us looking for what we can get out of the other.
Our appetites are often satisfied at the expense of those around us.
In a dog-eat-dog world we lose part of our humanity.

Jon Foreman[2]

At the beginning of the twentieth century Sigmund Freud's work on psychology and psychoanalysis became popular among ruling elites across the West. Freud explored the unconscious forces at play within the human psyche and viewed them as a continual threat to our rationality and emotional stability. In his words, 'every civilization must be built upon the coercion and renunciation of instinct'.[3] Freud referred to our natural instinct, that part of our psyche that corresponds to Nature, as the 'id' – our instinctual id-body. For him, this id-body was chaotic and wild – 'a cauldron full of seething excitations'.[4] Freud was building on a long taken philosophical understanding (exacerbated by the Enlightenment's 'Age of Reason') that our nature was essentially irrational and so our rational mind needed to control our irrational body. His views on social psychology – which were influenced by the individualism of Gustave Le Bon and Thomas Hobbes before him – assumed the main driver for social agency was individual self-interest.[5]

In the United States of America, during the 1920s, Edward Bernays, Freud's cousin, became a pioneer in post-war propaganda for social planning in what he termed 'public relations'. He used psychological theory for social planning as he perceived that people were innately irrational and self-serving and so needed to be manipulated in order for a stable, democratic society to work effectively. Public relations used psychological information gathered from university studies and extensive focus-group research to gain an understanding of people's desires. Public relations used celebrity advertising, placements in films and such like to influence certain desires with the aim of placating the masses. Citizens became consumers to pacify and stabilise in order to ensure effective governing of a largely irrational populace. Democracy with a sinister undertone of social manipulation formed. According to Bernays, 'The conscious and intelligent manipulation of the organized habits and opinions of the masses is an important element in democratic society.'[6]

On Black Tuesday – October 29, 1929 – the stock market crashed, plunging North America and Europe into protracted recession. Angry mobs took to the streets on both sides of the Atlantic. With this backdrop, the Nazi movement gathered momentum in Germany in the 1930s. In America, Roosevelt did not share Bernays' view that people were inherently irrational and self-serving; Roosevelt believed people would strive to be good citizens if society strived to be just and fair. With Roosevelt in power (1933) Bernays and his approach to public relations fell from grace. Instead Roosevelt embarked on a programme of government infrastructure investment called 'The New Deal' to help revive the economy and reduce unemployment. Yet this public sector initiative made little room for the private sector, which had become a powerful force. Big business did not like the Roosevelt administration's overriding commitment to fiscal policy and state investment and so hired Bernays to create a vision of American society where it was 'corporate America' which brought wealth, prosperity and happiness to the people rather than the state. Bernays helped develop the vision of free-market capitalism where citizens became consumers, having their desires met by corporations. Consumer capitalism was born, where demand is manipulated to stimulate economic growth. As the economist Victor Lebow famously stated:

> Our enormously productive economy ... demands that we make consumption our way of life, that we convert the buying and using of goods into rituals, that we seek our spiritual satisfaction, our ego satisfaction, in consumption ... We need things consumed, burned up, worn out, replaced, and discarded at an ever increasing rate.[7]

After the atrocities of the Second World War, there was an increasing concern among the ruling classes that people were fundamentally irrational and so could not be trusted. If democracy was to survive, they thought, the masses needed to be manipulated through social planning. Freudian psychoanalysis in the late 1940s and 50s became mainstream in American society, gaining widespread popularity in Europe too. In America, public relations for both government and business came back in favour. The CIA and other institutions invested in psychoanalysis research to understand the needs, wants and desires of the American public. Adam Curtis in his illuminating BBC documentary, *The Century of the Self,* explores how both government and big business shared an interest in social planning to maintain democracy through manipulation. This shared interest helped form a new ruling elite in America as senior government and corporate decision-makers viewed consumerism as the solution to their common challenge. Paradoxically, psychoanalysis, initially designed for personal liberation, became applied for social constraint. The Cold War in the 1950s and 60s gave additional fear-based justification for continued investment into psychological research for social planning purposes.

During the sixties the American anti-war movement, along with student protests against corporate America, caused much concern amongst the ruling elite. Self-actualisation was gaining popularity among the educated public rather than the pursuit of happiness through brand identification and material status. This self-actualisation trend became an important influence in American society as well as in Western Europe, and it started to impact on consumer patterns. There was a concern that corporate profits could fall when supply of their products outstripped consumer demand if people's desire to consume waned. Cleverly, according to Curtis, the public relations engine of corporate America supported by state-funded research manipulated the desire for personal freedom and individuality into the preoccupation of material self-expression. Capitalism helped these people express their individuality through consumerism. Self-actualisation became debased by egotistic self-expression with selfishness and greed fed by, and in turn feeding, consumerism.

In the 1970s public relations had to become more sophisticated as self-expressive individuals were more difficult to categorise into the traditional consumer types used for public relations activities. Following rigorous research undertaken by the Stanford Research Institute and others into the desires, wishes, values and inner-directives of these individuals, it was found that self-expressive people could be categorised through 'life-styles' where personal satisfaction, values and a sense of freedom are considered more important than social status. To predict people's consumer behaviour based on life-style types meant understanding how their values or inner-directives related to their self-expression. This research was used to get Ronald Reagan (1981) and Margaret Thatcher (1979) into power in America and Britain through political campaigns appealing to the inner-directives of people wishing for a sense of personal freedom and liberation from government intervention.

Throughout the 1980s in America and Britain both politics and big business engaged in further extensive research to understand the values and life-styles of the public and how consumption and voting patterns related to the psychological desires of different categories of people within society. The corporations managed to keep demand outstripping supply through clever advertising, creating associations of certain products and services to certain life-styles which became self-fuelling as the more people of that life-style associated with the products and services, the stronger the association became. Celebrity culture formed an important part of ensuring demand was continually propped up by artificial desires. This has led to the situation which Robert Hamilton, author of the book *Earthdream,* points to as an artificial 'good life' which debases us of our true nature and authenticity:

> Instead of learning to cultivate an identity through our inner potentiality, through the natural expression of our humanity, we are conditioned to manufacture an identity in outer appearances, most commonly through achieving material 'success' – the capitalist touchstone of the 'good life'. Lacking a solid individual sense of our own existence, our identity comes to be rooted in our self-worth, validated externally in terms of what we own and what people think of us.[8]

Tony Blair's New Labour (1997) in Britain and the Clinton administration (1993) in America came to power on the back of public relations driving political campaigns aimed at winning over the middle classes by changing their party's socialist policies to align more with those of individualism. Politics was no longer about leadership, vision or policy, but about power and manipulation, just as business became about the maximisation of short-term returns for shareholders rather than value-creation for stakeholders. As Hamilton points out we find ourselves in a bizarre reality where:

> Votes are won by pandering to people's greed, not by appealing to their ideals. Consequently, modern politics has far more to do with kowtowing to short-term vested interests than any kind of long term planning.[9]

The political theorist Colin Crouch, amongst others, notes that we now live in a post-democratic age where popular demands are manipulated by political elites.[10] Truly representative democracy is in crisis with many political theorists pointing to separateness – fuelled by an individualistic and highly competitive ideology – as the cause.[11]

Consumerism gives the illusion of self-determination by playing up to and satisfying our fickle desires of the egotistic self. Hollow whims taken from focus group research are then magnified through sophisticated public relations, advertising and marketing media. Purchasing products we don't really need is 'good' for the economy; the more consumers spend the better. This perpetuation of egotism rather than authenticity ensures the insatiable desires of the consumer are never truly satisfied. Our consumerist socio-economic paradigm is rooted in illusion; perpetuating the illusion allows us to remain fragmented from sources of real happiness. As the psychoanalyst and social theorist Joel Kovel notes: 'Were people either happy or clear about what they wanted, then capital's ceaseless expansion would be endangered.'[12]

The Debt Mountain

After the bursting of the dot com bubble, the administration of George W. Bush and the Federal Reserve's Alan Greenspan sought to stimulate economic growth through the quick-fix of easy credit, while largely overlooking the deeper structural challenges facing the American economy. From 2001 to 2003 Greenspan reduced interest rates from

6.5% to 1% (their lowest since 1961). This began an unprecedented consumer binge throughout the West, fuelling house-price rises and consumer debt. This short-term quick-fix can be likened to a heroin addict injecting another high to obscure the deeper malaise. The party atmosphere warms up nicely, due to easy money, yet is unsustainable. No real lasting contribution to the advancement of society or the world at large is generated from such consumerism, in fact quite the opposite. Much like the drug addict inflicts psychological and biological harm through the abusive use of drugs and the anti-social, self-destructive behaviours that come with it, so too does the consumer-fuelled high lead to social and environmental damage as well as economic ill-health in the long run. The consumerist high distracts us from dealing with the real challenges and opportunities life affords us.

Lower interest rates, higher consumer spending, house-price bubbles, higher personal debt – these are all the unsustainable economic factors that led to the almighty crash of 2007, the party's hangover which left so many people badly affected. Yet at the time of writing this in 2014, all these unsustainable economic factors are back in vogue, the party is being revved up again. We seem averse to learning the error of our ways and desperate to keep on masking over the cracks of our deeper corruptions. As at 2014, Britain has an unprecedented sovereign and personal debt mountain. It is personal debt that has become the main fuel for 'household consumption'. House price rises help give householders a 'feel-good factor' even amid falling year-on-year real earnings (the amount these households earn in real terms beyond inflation). And so the consumer goes out and spends more while saving less, saddling themselves with more debt. To help put this debt accumulation into some sort of historic perspective, George W. Bush accumulated more debt as President than all the other Presidents of the United States put together. President Obama is fast exceeding Bush's record.

Along with the meteoric rise of consumerism has come the general erosion of public provision for housing, pensions, medical care, education, utilities and other services in both Britain and America. Many other Western countries have followed suit to greater or lesser degrees. Today in Britain young adults leave university saddled with debts; then to come are the mortgage and credit card repayments. To escape debt-slavery these days is more and more difficult. It is increasingly challenging for people to follow any authentic calling in their work as priority is given to jobs that pay well enough to support a life-style that fits within the consumerist culture. As the psychologist Andy Fisher explains:

> We are born into a social world in which our need for personal viability or security gets 'met' by being twisted down along narrow economic pathways which then become difficult to leave, for both emotional and structural reasons. We are just too existentially vulnerable for it to be otherwise, at least for most of us. These pathways, however, fail to bring us the release from fear we desire.[13]

In Britain the use of anti-depressants has increased fivefold in the last two decades and now at least one in ten Western teenage girls suffer from anorexia.[14] We find ourselves living immersed within a socio-economic system that stifles our greatness for creativity, community and love while exploiting our weakness through greed, jealousy and fear. The corrosive effects of debt-fuelled economics, is becoming more widely recognised. For instance, Michael Rawbothan, in his book *The Grip of Death,* provides an exemplary exploration of how the Western approach of debt-based finance catalyses an increasingly ferocious need to compete, engendering widespread tensions and divisions across society, while eroding the co-operative venture and deeper sense of purpose our work ought to provide.[15] In short, debt-based consumerism enslaves and debases both worker and consumer. When discussing the whys and wherefores of this corrupting socio-economic system, Rawbothan does not point to a conspiracy of powerful elites seeking control over the masses, rather he points to an ignorance and arrogance sown deep within the philosophical mindset of the well-educated in business and government. For Rawbothan, it is a flawed philosophy of control-based thinking with hierarchic, monopolistic, hyper-competitive tendencies. This philosophy, he argues, has become an ingrained tyranny, corrupting democracy itself.[16] It is this flawed mindset which the pages ahead seek to tackle, as any transformation in socio-economics without an accompanying change in attitude will not last long.

In the next chapter we explore how the ideology of individualism, capitalist consumerism and socio-economic control was influenced by a perception of life itself being individualistic, self-serving and highly competitive.

2. A Dog-Eat-Dog World

The whole philosophy of Hell rests on a recognition of the axiom that one thing is not another thing, and, specifically, that one self is not another self … .it means the sucking of will and freedom out of a weaker self into a stronger. 'To be' means 'to be in competition'.

C.S. Lewis[1]

Our prevalent worldview is that we inhabit a purposeless, accidental and materialistic universe. After the spontaneous Big Bang, some fourteen billion years ago, inert matter exploded throughout the space-time void without purpose or direction. Matter then interacted – through the mechanistic push/pull forces prescribed by Newtonian physics – and coalesced to form the galaxies and solar systems we view through our telescopes today. Life on Earth started some 3.8 billion years ago when biological life spontaneously emerged from an accidental gathering of chemical building blocks electrified within the primordial soup. Life just happened because by some extraordinarily improbable quirk of fate there were the right conditions for it to do so and it then set about struggling for existence by competing with itself ever since.

Ecology is the study of relationships and interactions of living things in their environment. While ancient Greek philosophers such as Hippocrates and Aristotle laid the foundations of Western ecology, today's evolutionary ecology is largely built upon Neo-Darwinian principles of competition and separation. These principles define the organism, and ultimately the gene, as an independent unit of evolution struggling for existence against a prevailingly hostile environment. In this Neo-Darwinian view of evolutionary ecology, all creativity in life comes about through random mutations filtered through natural selection: a struggle against the odds with no purpose other than to exist. It is hard to gain any sense of enchantment or gratitude for such a pointless life, yet this is what we have been teaching ourselves to believe, a story extrapolated from Darwin's seminal work published in 1859 entitled *The Origin of Species by Means of Natural Selection or the Preservation of Favoured Races in the Struggle for Life.*[2]

The twin pillars of Darwinism

Darwinian evolution is premised upon two basic tenets that form what he termed 'natural selection': first, survival of the fittest; second, random variation.

Survival of the fittest

As a biological model of evolution, survival of the fittest assumes that variant forms are weeded out through a process of elimination within the struggle of existence. It is worth pointing out that back in 1859 when Darwin used the word 'fittest' he did not mean what we mean today by the word fittest as in strongest, leanest or smartest, he meant the organism's ability to fit in to its pre-existing environment. Those fitting best by being most adapted to the conditions imposed by their environment were best able to survive.

In effect, the concept of 'environment' is here envisaged as a set of 'locks' – known as 'niches' – and life forms are envisaged as a random assortment of 'keys' that are required to fit in (conform with or adapt) to the locks. Well-fitting keys 'win', less well-fitting keys 'lose' until eventually only the 'best fit' remain via a process known as 'competitive exclusion'. That the keys themselves might have anything to do with shaping the locks is not taken into account because they are regarded, in effect, as independent, randomly generated entities (statistical randomness means independent occurrence) – that is, as 'content' separate from 'context'.

Social Darwinism, conceptualised initially by Herbert Spencer in 1903, focused on survival of the fittest as a theory for human societal development. It was founded on the premise that some people can be viewed as dominant, fitter and superior over other inferior, weaker people. It helped justify colonialism by viewing invaders as superior to the indigenous natives and so survival of the fittest being played out; the dominant race winning out over the inferior one.

Likewise, it also helped the justification of eugenic programmes in the United States in the early twentieth century which proposed the weeding out of unfit genes in the population; it also helped justify Nazi Germany's ethnic cleansing in Europe. Still today the prevalent view in corporate business is one of 'dog-eat-dog' competitiveness rooted in Social Darwinist elitism where businesses colonise new markets; the dominant company winning out over the inferior one. It is an approach seldom questioned and yet its mindset is dreadfully inadequate and deeply divisive. The deeper we understand how life actually evolves on Earth the more we realise neither antagonistic competition nor even coercive co-operation can actually drive evolution in the world we see around us.

Random variation

Random variation is the second pillar upon which Darwinism is founded, and in modern times is attributed to genetic mutation. Mutations are changes in the genetic sequence of an organism which bring about a subsequent change in the organism which may or may not notably improve or reduce its ability to sustain itself. The concept of random mutation is that these genetic changes happen as random mistakes in the genetic processing of the organism. It is pure chance as to whether the mutated organism happens to benefit or not from the mistake. As a result evolution, within this theory, happens incrementally over long durations and eventually stalls if there is no accompanying environmental change. If, for whatever reason, environmental conditions do change, some of the random mistakes prove beneficial and so act like fortuitous adaptations. The organisms that happened to chance by such favourable mutations improve their ability to survive and propogate; slowly but surely the mutants become the favoured variants.

In 1972, Gould and Eldredge published a theory of punctuated evolution. This theory explores how evolutionary leaps could occur. Long periods (millions of years) of relatively little change are followed by short periods (thousands of years) of transformation. Orthodox thinking now assumes that the Darwinian mechanism of adaptation takes place largely in these long periods of minor adaptation and that during these 'punctuated' periods, changes in the dynamics between organisms and the environment break down and then break through as a transformative process takes over. During this transformative period the environment enters a chaos-like state known as bifurcation. During bifurcation the interplay of relationships between organisms and the environment are reconfigured and a fundamentally new ecological situation emerges with new relationships that find relative order within their environmental context. Darwin's evolutionary theory appears to explain aspects of piecemeal, incremental changes in species but does little to explain the transformative leaps we know have occurred throughout history and that indeed happen in our own human societies.

Even in terms of the piecemeal, incremental changes outside of these periods of punctuated evolution, evidence of life evolving in similar yet genetically disparate ways suggests it is increasingly unlikely that small random mutations and natural selection alone can produce the complexity of life we witness around us. Biologist Brian Goodwin, for instance, points to an inherent pattern to life which is deeper than any purely functional or accidental pattern. Even Darwin himself questioned how random mutation could account for all variation:

> To suppose that the eye with all its inimitable contrivances for adjusting the focus to different distances, for admitting different amounts of light, and for the correction of spherical and chromatic aberration, could have been formed by natural selection, seems, I freely confess, absurd in the highest degree.[3]

Neo-Darwinism

Since the 1970s the Neo-Darwinian doctrine has become the dominant evolutionary paradigm. Neo-Darwinism provides a clear-cut set of rules for evolution with all the comforting sense of security that brings. As a doctrine, it has magnified aspects of Darwin's theory while de-emphasising other aspects. Neo-Darwinism seeks to explain evolution through what it views as its building blocks – genes. Richard Dawkins is a well-known Neo-Darwinian scientist and author of *The Selfish Gene* amongst other books. Dawkins recognises the indispensable influence environment has on life; he also recognises that genes which cooperate well with other genes do better than those that don't and notes that we are gigantic colonies of symbiotic genes.[4] Yet for Dawkins, in true Neo-Darwinian style, he concludes by assuming that the gene only cooperates due to its own self-centred gain. He recognises that a number of different species cooperate through partnerships – like the flower and bee, the aphid and ant, the fungus and algae – but for him such prevalent symbiotic behaviour is always due to underlying selfish motives. For Dawkins, life is nothing but competitive struggle, even if sometimes the struggle is played out through partnerships and networks, the motive is always one of competition and exploitation.

All the time new findings bring fresh perspective to how we view the evolution of life. Far from the genome being a rigid set of building blocks we realise it is a fluid system of dynamic localities that evolve by interplaying with the environment. We recognise that evolution is essentially co-creative, fluid and variably connective. Rather than organisms simply struggling for survival they struggle, flourish and thrive through dynamic relationships. As anyone in a marriage will know – or eventually find out – relationships are dynamic, multifaceted and immersed within a diverse matrix of wider relations.

The original corruption

The anthropologist-philosopher Gregory Bateson viewed Darwin's theory of evolution as fundamentally flawed because it is based on the organism as the unit of evolution rather than the organism *and* its relationship with its environment. This definition of the organism as separate from its environment Bateson saw as a basic flaw which corrupts the thinking that flows from it, as for him relationships are paramount to the organism's health, viability and evolution. He viewed comparing one species against another or versus its environment in a struggle for survival as inherently wrong. He felt that it is what pits humanity against Nature and provides for our prevalent worldview of survival through competition, in what he viewed as 'an ecology of bad ideas', breeding parasitic humans, purely self-centred and destructive of their host environment.

For Bateson this flawed worldview deeply acculturates us to the notion of 'self' and 'species' as separate from our environment.[5] This separation of content from context – which encourages a perceived separation of humans from Nature – creates a disharmonious way of living with our environment where we foolishly seek to subversively control it, bizarrely blaming it for our disharmony. Bateson viewed this separation as extracting humans from the Mind of Nature, the 'Ecology of Mind' as he called it. To separate the human mind from that of Nature, and also to separate mind from body or intellect from emotions is an error of the most fundamental degree which Bateson saw as woven into Western habits of thought at deep and partly unconscious levels.[6] He laid the blame for this original corruption at the foot of Western rationalism, and its reductionist tendencies, viewing much of it as insane while viewing Eastern philosophy and its notion of attuning with Nature's wisdom as far wiser.

Excessive competition

The creature that wins against its environment destroys itself.
                                                    Gregory Bateson[7]

This corrupt worldview, which separates humans from Nature, values aspects of Nature that provide human benefit in some way. Anything that is not perceived as quantifiably beneficial to humanity as a food source, supporter of food, commodity ingredient, servant provider of labour or some tourist or aesthetic benefit is perceived as having no value. If other life forms use sources of human benefit in a way that affects their value to humans, like eating crops, then they are viewed as competitive 'threats' to be eradicated: predators, parasites, 'pests' or 'weeds'.

The word 'eradicate' is used here rather than 'kill', because it is in our cultural history not to just kill those life forms immediately challenging us or our sources of benefit at that moment in time but to strategically target, poison, weed-out or hunt down, sometimes even destroying their homes and killing their young. This is one area where 'civilised' human beings radically differ from indigenous peoples and from the rest of non-human life. It is exceptionally rare to find other species eradicating perceived threats in such a determined and all-encompassing way. The problem with this excessively competitive approach to life is that it leads to the destruction of inhabitants vital to the sustainable functioning of naturally diverse communities. When other life forms arrive to inhabit the vacancy left gaping from eradication, or become rampant because their own rivals have been wiped out, then we set about trying to control or cull these life forms too, often using methods of life-destruction that impact on others, for instance, chemical sprays, poisons or man-made diseases. Natural communities become more and more damaged as a result of this corrupt approach.

Civilised Western organisations and societies often take a similarly highly-competitive approach in their collective and individual behaviour, not necessarily in the extreme case of eradicating other humans (although that has happened on numerous occasions to the detriment of indigenous people and ethnic minorities, for instance) but in their approach to competing through domination of markets and sources of potential benefit. This is the mindset that underpins 'dog-eat-dog' capitalism, the dominant socio-economic logic of the West.

Daniel Quinn in his book *Ishmael* explains the problem of this excessive competition well by explaining that the 'law of competition' in Nature says you may compete but you may not wage war:

> If competitors hunted each other down just to make them dead, then there would be no competitors. There would simply be one species at each level of competition: the strongest ... The lion defends its kill as its own, but it doesn't defend the herd as its own ... Bees will deny you access to what's inside their hive in the apple tree, but they won't deny you access to the apples.[8]

Excessive systemic competition, he goes on to say, is dangerous to the fabric of life and in turn to humanity. 'You end up with a community in which diversity is progressively destroyed in order to support the expansion of a single species.'[9]

The demise of diversity

Biodiversity and cultural diversity have shaped one another over the millennia, as we curtail diversity through excessive competition and control we undermine our culture's resilience. Life ought to be about celebrating variety, choice and diversity and yet within our Western mindset we seek to conform, normalise and homogenise where possible which goes hand-in-hand with diminishing life's creative potential. The environmentalist Vandana Shiva points to a 'monoculture of the mind' that poisons our culture, in turn poisoning everything we attend to.[10] While 'free markets' are touted as the cornerstone of capitalism, in reality creative freedom is converted into private property where possible: intellectual creativity (such as innovation) and biological creativity (such as genetically diverse seeds) are patented and monopolised. Our social and biological resilience so dependent on diversity is traded-in for control. As Prince Charles, HRH The Prince of Wales notes, 'Nature displays a tendency towards variety and away from uniformity and yet we seem to be heading in the opposite direction.'[11] Put simply, this excessively competitive approach to life sows the seeds of its own demise by undermining its evolutionary potential; the cancer ends up destroying itself.

In the next chapter we explore the philosophical and scientific logic that formed in the period of time leading up to Darwin's work in order to shed light on how certain ways of thinking came to dominate.

3. The Cartesian Separation

[We have] a sufficiently strong propensity not only to make divisions in knowledge where there are none in nature, and then to impose the divisions on nature, making the reality thus comfortable to the idea, but to go further, and to convert the generalisations made from observation into positive entities, permitting for the future these artificial creations to tyrannise over the understanding.

Henry Maudsley[1]

Up to the late sixteenth and early seventeenth century, Catholicism, natural philosophy and ancient Hermetic traditions blended with Neo-Platonism, paganism and Aristotelian-Scholastic traditions to allow for vestiges of the ancient belief in the divine immanence of Nature to exist alongside a transcendent God. The natural world was viewed as exhibiting a World Soul, or *anima mundi*. Yet Europe was then in a time of great upheaval. Plagues and famines as well as the Thirty Years' War (1618–48) followed on from the break-up of the Church through the Reformation. The rise of Protestantism, rationalism and empiricism started to alter the worldview of Nature as divine towards a view that God was divorced from nature (Nature then became nature with a small 'n', de-spirited, de-animated, without World Soul). The Middle Ages, with its embedded beliefs, cultural ways and mindsets gave way to a new worldview. The great minds of the period – Francis Bacon, Galileo Galilei, Johannes Kepler, Thomas Hobbes, René Descartes, and many others – built upon the transformative and revolutionary climate of the Renaissance to form the Age of Enlightenment which witnessed the Scientific Revolution and then the Industrial Revolution with profound effects on the Western world, greatly accelerating our ability to transform our environment for better or worse.[2] Of particular relevance for us here is the rise of scientific positivism and the de-sacralising effect it had on our Western way of attending.

The de-sacralisation of Nature

Friar Marin Mersenne, Pierre Gassendi and others in the early seventeenth century made concerted efforts to 'cleanse' the Church and State from pagan and Neo-Platonic perspectives which celebrated the sacredness of the natural world. Gassendi explained that the existence of psyche or soul in Nature is beyond what can be empirically verified, defined and quantified and so of questionable value as its factual correctness is unproven. The science historian Morris Berman suggests Gassendi's critique on the existence of a World Soul may be the earliest known statement of scientific positivism.[3] This is the school of thought that soon became the leading doctrine of the West. It states that only verifiable facts attained through rational deductive reasoning and empirical measurements can be understood as truths; in other words the only truth is objectified scientific knowledge.

The views of Mersenne and Gassendi that God was not a World Soul but an external Ruler of creation influenced, amongst others, René Descartes who is widely regarded as the most influential philosopher of the Enlightenment. On the night of November 10, 1619, in a dream that profoundly transformed the young Frenchman, Descartes conceived of the universe as a gigantic machine.[4] He understood his life's mission as developing a comprehensive natural philosophy, a new vision of the natural world. Descartes was a first-rate mathematician and he applied this mathematical mind to understanding the workings of the universe which, for Descartes, were all explainable through mathematical propositions. Clearly, the view that everything throughout the universe could be explained, measured and defined had a powerful allure. Descartes then applied this mechanistic concept to humanity; he wrote, 'All of these functions unfold naturally in this machine (the body) by virtue of the arrangement of its organs, just like clockwork.'[5] Descartes along with Mersenne and Gassendi felt compelled to repudiate the notion of Nature as living, psychic and sentient. In 1630, he wrote to Mersenne saying, 'God sets up mathematical laws in nature, as a king sets up laws in his kingdom.'[6] Descartes famously set about excluding any mind-like consciousness from Nature leaving it inert with his 'mind-body' dualism, where mind is viewed as separate from matter. Nature separated from mind was the necessary precondition for the objectivity of modern scientific positivism. Rather than imbued with divine sentience, 'nature' came to be perceived as chunks of matter; building blocks that collided and coalesced through deterministic push-pull forces definable through the abstract rationality of mathematical propositions. Other great minds of the Enlightenment, such as Thomas Hobbes and Francis Bacon, contributed to the rise of scientific positivism by focusing on empirical observation and rational mathematical logic as the way to ascertain truth. Notably, Hobbes' basic assumption was that humanity and nature consist of atomised, competitive units embroiled in a 'war of all against all'.[7] The political philosophy of Hobbes profoundly influenced many great minds after him including those of Bernays and Freud.

By the 1650s, key figures in the Royal Society of London, the Montmor Academy in France, and later the reorganised French Academy of Science, championed the notion of a 'value-free' science based solely on proven fact through empirical experiment and rational deductive logic. Modern science was founded upon the materialistic notion of a de-spirited mechanistic worldview. This modern spirit-free science went hand-in-hand with the advent of Protestantism. The Neo-Platonic and pagan notions of God's immanence within Nature came to be perceived as 'evil magic' to be dispelled. The last vestiges of sacred Nature which had coexisted within Catholicism from the outset of Christianity in the form of accepted paganism were banished from the dominant worldview. Humanity's participation within Nature through its divine immanence was withdrawn, and science heralded the dogmatic belief in dualism: Man as the son of God was perceived as apart from nature; nature was no longer imbued with divinity, on the contrary it became viewed as 'impure'. The way to God was 'upwards' through the transcendent realm not within the impurity of a de-spirited nature which was to be viewed as nothing more than a material collection of objects to be managed and manipulated for human betterment.

Truth was no longer a dynamic unfolding found through a participatory experiential embodiment of Nature, it became a static truth defined by dissecting an object from its lived-in context and analysing it through experiments supported by mathematical logic; this is referred to as the 'objectification' of science. By its nature, this objectification is abstract because things are taken out of their lived-in context, defined through abstract logic and examined through repeatable experiments in controlled abstract environments.

The direct embodied experience of the observer along with any intuitive feelings are split aside, perceived as fickle 'subjectivity', from the supposedly dependable 'objectivity' of standing apart from the phenomenon. This 'abstract rationality' or 'rationalism' explicitly involves a standing apart from Nature rather than an embodied participation within it. Scientific experiment, which was meant to be exploring reality, actually became controlled to constrain the variable qualities of real life. These abstract experimental designs using abstract mathematical logic enforce a predictable, measurable linearity on to what is otherwise non-linear and unpredictable. This ensured neat, definable 'answers' could be found through an abstract version of truth. A powerfully convenient (yet artificial) assumption of separation allowed us to dissect and examine all we analysed in a way that is now referred to as 'Cartesian science' after Descartes himself; a deeply woven assumption ingrained in Western scientific-philosophy to this day.

By the second half of the eighteenth century, the majority of Europe's leading establishments had fallen in line with this alluring modern scientific outlook. Everything in the world and cosmos beyond, it was assumed, could be understood, defined, measured and so eventually manipulated by humanity. God's grand design was there to be understood by humanity for humanity, who – as the chosen species – had dominion over all aspects of His creation. Theory-based rationalistic explanation verified by repeatable, systematic empiricism was the major innovation of the Enlightenment. This innovation was profound and enabled the great feats of techno-science that triggered the Industrial Revolution and the subsequent transformation this has had on our Western world.

The Cartesian worldview of content as separable from context and of the individual human psyche as separable from a de-sacralised nature helped set up dualism and the fragmenting splits this incurs throughout Western thought. Hundreds of years of collective thinking in this way have had a restrictive effect on our logic and perspective, deeply affecting our culture, science, language, governance and philosophy. It is hard to feel a sense of engagement with Nature when our perspective of it is seen through an objectifying lens perceiving a mechanistic, soulless world. Abstract rationality as part of an inclusive way of attending is an important part of reasoning, yet when skewed into nothing but rationalism winds up distorting reality. For instance, how is spontaneous creativity – an ingredient so fundamental to life – explained through this objectifying lens? As Albert Einstein himself noted, 'As far as the laws of mathematics refer to reality, they are not certain, and as far as they are certain, they do not refer to reality.'[8]

Western dualism

With Cartesian science firmly embedded into our Western culture, our way of attending became increasingly through our rational minds, dismembered from our sensuous bodies and our intuitive hearts. Our participatory way of relating with life became increasingly narrowed down and desensitised. This encourages a polarised perspective of reality – in both our internal and external worlds – for instance, body or spirit, order or chaos, quantifiable or unquantifiable, masculine or feminine, matter or space, rational or irrational, conscious or unconscious, human or nature, self or other, something or nothing, life or death, good or evil, and so on. The polarising of life's rich and colourful continua into discrete either/or separations of their extreme poles (black or white) is called 'dualism'. The rational abstraction of content from context – so essential for objectification – is at the root of these artificial binary selections. This dualistic outlook is not so much the product of the rational as the abuse of the rational – due to a mechanism of abstract separation imposed on reality – and reason itself may be called upon to question and correct it.

Such a dualistic way of attending affects how we interpret and relate with life, infecting our relationship with ourselves, each other and all of life. We are brought up with it, schooled in it and find our way of living within it, and so our collective and individual belief-systems are steeped in it. For instance, the Freudian splitting of 'ego' from natural 'wildness' (id) is a quite different perspective to a natural self-identity readily permeating with its embodied neighbourhood correspondingly including and caring for natural wildness instead of egoistically seeking dominion over it. In this healthier situation, the conscious and unconscious are seen as conversing and permeating as opposed to splitting and then vying for control. Likewise, the Neo-Darwinian separation of organism from its environment is quite a different perspective to an organism which readily permeates with its surroundings through a variety of exchanging relations instead of solely competing with and so seeking to dominate its environment.

De-naturing and the left/right brain hemispheres

Through extensively studying philosophy, neurology and neuropsychology, Iain McGilchrist synthesises that the type of world we find ourselves in relates to the relationship between the left and right brain hemispheres. According to his view, it would seem that, first off, the right hemisphere sees the world in its global context, then the left hemisphere grasps at this right hemisphere contextualisation bringing it into acute focus so atomised parts of it can be analysed. In so doing, the parts being focused on are re-presented in a lifeless, decontextualised way; the parts are 'de-natured'. The right hemisphere then re-constitutes what the left hemisphere has processed and so replaces the atomised left hemisphere view back into a natural, real-life context. If, for some reason, the right-left-right hemispheric working relationship is disturbed so that the final reconstituting stage of the right hemisphere does not complete the left's atomised, de-natured view, then the world for us would change into something quite different: an abstract, fragmented, atomised worldview which is disembodied, lacking contextual insight.[9] The left hemisphere with its grasping, competitive and power-hungry manner, McGilchrist argues, has done just that, it has increased its hold over its narrow-minded view causing its worldview to become primary with the right hemisphere's intuitive perception becoming secondary. We explore this left/right brain hemispheric relationship further in Chapter Six.

To summarise, the Cartesian dualism of our prevailing scientific paradigm quests for clarity of understanding through absoluteness. This noble search for understanding goes some way in satisfying our 'making sense' desire and material manipulation of reality yet obscures and deludes by constructing an artificial reality of narrowed down conformity. In 'making sense' we, ironically, desensitise ourselves from the ever-changing world we experience. We construct logical boundaries to help our understanding, and yet in the process we close ourselves off from truly making sense. We create an illusion of separation that then deludes and imprisons us. In Part Two we explore some alternative approaches to dualistic rationalism gaining interest in the West which aid our ability to break free from this imprisonment. In the next chapter we continue our exploration by venturing further upstream to the formation of Western philosophy in search of the whys and wherefores of this flawed logic.

4. The Formation of Western Philosophy

The word 'philosophy' originates from the ancient Greek *philo,* meaning to love and *Sophia,* the goddess of wisdom, hence philosophy originally meant the love of wisdom.[1] As the writer Henry David Thoreau explained, a philosopher does not merely think subtle thoughts but loves wisdom so as to live the wisdom through simplicity, authenticity and integrity.[2]

The intriguing history of Western philosophy tends to be categorised as follows:

◊ Presocratic philosophy of ancient Greece – the founders of Western philosophy in ancient Greece from the seventh and sixth centuries BC up to Socrates' death in 399 BC.

◊ Post-Socratic Hellenistic and Roman period – from Plato through to the spread of Christianity in the fourth century AD.

◊ Medieval Philosophy – from the spread of Christianity in the fourth century and the collapse of the Western Roman Empire in the fifth century through to the Renaissance period commencing in Italy in the fourteenth century. Over the centuries, Roman and Greek philosophy became integrated with Christian theology.

◊ The Renaissance – fourteenth to early seventeenth century transformations in philosophy, culture, education, art and science.

◊ Early Modern Philosophy – beginning with the Scientific Revolution and Church Reformation of the sixteenth century, then the Age of Enlightenment of the mid-seventeenth and eighteenth century and into the Industrial Revolution of the late eighteenth centuries.

◊ Modern Day philosophy – nineteenth century onwards.

The Pre-socratics

The epic poems of Homer from eighth century BC Greece found their home in a cultural melting pot. The remnants of the indigenous Neolithic European customs and rituals blended with the patriarchal cultures of the different waves of invaders from the Indus, Steppes and Middle East. Greek mysticism – Orphic, Dionysian, Eleusinian – evolved from these indigenous and oriental origins. The Homeric rhapsodies lived within the oral culture of eighth century BC Greece, being played out through ritual enactment or chanted by bards. Yet over the next couple of centuries, the take up of the alphabet and written word by the Greeks had a profound effect on Western philosophical discourse. It affected the art of storytelling, the rhythm of communal life and the instinctive, poetic, inter-personal and embodied ways of attending to life. During this time of immense change, the relation to land and property also changed as did the ways in which land-based communities and urban societies organised themselves. The Pre-socratic philosophers of the seventh and sixth century BC found themselves amidst this cultural upheaval.

From the Homeric poems through to Socrates the theme running through Pre-socratic philosophy is attuning with the wisdom of the divine order so as to perceive reality beyond illusion. Thales, Pythagoras and Democritus are often viewed as the fathers of Western philosophy and science. Western thought is often portrayed as starting with Thales' rejection of purely supernatural phenomena to explain reality, yet like Homer before him he perceived Nature and divinity as entwined. Pythagoras is said to have been the first person to call himself a 'lover of wisdom' – a philosopher. For him reason and religion combined, with spiritual illumination found through the soul. The mathematical and musical qualities of the natural order were expressions of the divine. Parmenides of Elea is often portrayed as the founding father of rational logic, yet this overlooks the primary essence of his teachings: to understand the divine is to venture beyond the rational mind. These great Pre-socratics were influenced by Persian, Egyptian and Arab ways of understanding, which in turn share conceptual thinking from sources further afield such as India, China and Japan, as well as the indigenous belief systems of Neolithic cultures. For instance Democritus, who formulated the atomic theory of the universe, was said to have had amongst his teachers a Persian alchemist magus called Ostanes. Pythagoras was linked to Orphic mysticism which was influenced by Persian, Hermetic and Eastern mysticism. Thales' understanding of the soul as mixed within the universal soul echoes Eastern mysticism and Heraclitus' view of everything as in a perpetual state of flux again resonates with Eastern mysticism and Neolithic animism.

These philosophers increasingly called upon the rational intellect to understand the natural order of things in relation to the divine. Yet their works were poetic, metaphorical, opaque and often misunderstood. In keeping with the mystical disciplines they drew from, they revealed their version of the divine truth in ways that could easily mislead those not ready or deeply aware enough to understand them. Notably Parmenides – as well as Empedocles, Zeno and others – used rational logic as a tool to shatter illusions of our reality, whereby he is so often referred to as the founder and upholder of rationalism. As Peter Kingsley points out in his book *Reality,* their teachings ask us to awaken an entirely different form of cognition than the rational mind can fathom: the perspective of immortality, the infinite and the Divine.[3] What they explored was the divinity of both Love and Strife beyond the illusion of separation. Their use of rational intellect has been singled out as the important essence of their work and so the essential purpose of the teachings of these great Pre-socratics is often misinterpreted.

Yet rationality was a tool increasingly used within Western philosophy for grasping the order of things. This search for order in the universe and the natural world formed the basis of ancient Greek philosophy, with the Greek word *kosmos* meaning 'order' as well as 'world' and 'universe'. Increasingly, the ancient Greek philosophers wished to discover the natural order through the rational mind. Democritus, for instance, viewed the subjective senses as important, yet for him it was the rational mind that could fathom the truth from 'illegitimate' aspects of subjectivity. Socrates, whose endeavour was human morality rather than universal ordering, believed that reason applied through dialectic debate was the way to find goodness, truth and justice for humanity *(dia* meaning 'through' and *legein* meaning 'to speak', in other words bringing reflection into speech so that opinion can be differentiated from real knowing). Socrates' dialectic process aims to bring the soul to actuality, restoring it to the original memory of divine Truth. For Socrates (and those before him) the cosmos itself is intelligible because it participates in mind or intellect. Thus there is a correspondence between the human soul and the cosmic intelligence. To know oneself and to know the cosmos are two aspects of one knowledge. This 'knowing' is the work of intellect, understood by Socrates as the highest faculty of the soul. The knowledge of the soul is the knowledge of the place of the soul within the universe, so that truth and goodness correspond through right action – the virtuous life. While rational argument became more prominent in Greek philosophy, this rationality as a tool within a deeper soulful intellect is quite different from the all-encompassing abstract rationality of positivist science explored in the previous chapter. 'Reason' and 'intellect' were core to the ancient Greeks, yet understood in a completely different way by the rationalists of the Scientific Revolution. For the Greeks and later for the medieval theologians and philosophers, 'reason' meant *ratio*, meaning the manner in which the mind gathers things in relation with each other. Reason commences in the plurality of things, seeking their order. 'Intellect' for the Greeks, on the other hand, has a primordial intuition of the order of the cosmos. Deductive and inductive modes of thought are connected with these two types of apprehension. Intellect thinks from eternal principles and discerns how these manifest in particulars, while reason ascends from particulars towards universals. The rationalism of the Scientific Revolution onwards is neither of these; it is the abstract reduction of content from context which mechanises reality by measuring fragments of it.

Stoic Philosophy

The Stoic school of philosophy was founded in Greece by Zeno (c.334–c.262 BC) and became highly influential throughout ancient Greek and then Roman elites. It largely surpassed the other two Hellenistic philosophical schools of Scepticisim and Epicureanism, maintaining dominance until sometime after the emperor Marcus Aurelius's death in AD 180 and the rise of Christianity in the third century. It was essentially a practical philosophy aimed at living rightly and in accordance with Nature. Stoics held that there was only one aim of philosophy, to live virtuously. This meant ruling the emotions and the will with reason. Reason discerned the divine order of the universe. Everything participates in this universal reason, including the human mind, and so any action was seen as either in harmony with, or contrary to, this divine order. So for the Stoics reason and virtue coincide with one another, since the virtuous life is in accordance with universal reason, and so Stoic philosophy is aimed at the practice of bringing the will and the emotions into harmony with the universal reason. None of the writings of Zeno have survived, but Cicero recounts much Stoic philosophy and in his *The Nature of the Gods* he writes, 'The universe itself is god and the universal outpouring of its soul; it is this same world's guiding principle, operating in mind and reason, together with the common nature of things and the totality that embraces all existence.'[4]

The advent of the written word

The Golden Age of Athens (500–400 BC) was a time of great transformation. The advent of the written word hand-in-hand with the rise of rational thought as a tool to define reality had a profound impact on the Western way of life. Let us take a moment here to explore the origins of language and the written word in Western culture.

The German philosopher Johann Herder explored the origins of language and found that originally language was not a code of representation but rather a generative creativity where the act of speaking was a participatory embodiment of the speaker within the lived-in environment; content as a participatory expression within context. The phonemic singing of language still evident in many indigenous cultures today seems to have its roots in music. The pictographic ideograms and hieroglyphics found in Egypt dating back some 3,000 BC, in China some 1,500 BC and in Mesoamerica around 600 BC enabled language to shift from purely oral to written and with that came a shift in sensory perception away from voice tones and body gestures very much within the sensory realm of the body to images.[5] Through syllables, concepts are represented in a way that the metaphoric essence of what is being expressed is relayed. These images portrayed the lived-in environment yet became more abstract in forming pictographic puns which invoked images that sound like the written explanation; the phonetic sound morphed into the written symbol. The sounds became transcribed as abstract content rather than the image of the content within its contextual meaning.[6] The Hebrews and Phoenicians adopted the alphabet and in time so did the ancient Greeks. The phonemic alphabet language is sequential and logical with consonants and vowels given specific meaning through words. During the eighth, seventh and sixth centuries BC, Greek was written in an alternating horizontal direction – a line of writing went one way, got to the end and then went back the other way, like ploughing a field. By the fifth century BC left to right on all lines of writing had become the norm. According to the neuroscientist Iain McGilchrist this left to right, horizontal, phonetic language greatly assisted left-brain hemisphere determination.[7] In his book *The Spell of The Sensuous,* cultural ecologist David Abram notes: 'With the advent of the aleph-beth, a new distance opens between human culture and the rest of nature.'[8] No longer did images relate to their animate context, the words had become abstract representations. The alphabet granted a new autonomy and permanence to abstract concepts enabling us to define things in an unchanging objectified way. This timeless yet abstract quality of the written word gives a sense of independence – perhaps even transcendence – from the ever-changing corporeal realm. Yet, as Ralph Waldo Emerson explains when discussing words, 'They cannot cover the dimensions of what is truth. They break, chop, and impoverish it.'[9] For McGilchrist, the alphabet and the widespread take up of currency over the same period, were not prime movers but rather epiphenomena of a deeper change already set in motion in Greek culture whereupon the left hemisphere came to dominate along with a shift in our way of attending.[10] In the midst of this came the influential philosophies of Plato and Aristotle.

Plato

Plato is central to Greek philosophy. He was Socrates' student and founder of the Academy in Athens. Fundamental to Platonic thought is the concept of Plato's Forms or Ideas. Forms in their ancient Greek context meant the patterns or essential qualities inherent within something. These Platonic Forms are the eternal transcendental qualities (such as Goodness, Beauty and Truth) that things in the world exhibit. These archetypal qualities are eternal as while the experience of the object being perceived may change, the archetypal quality is beyond ephemeral subjectivity or opinion – it is transcendent. Plato understood these Forms as the pure Truths which transcend the material, corporeal, temporal world. For Plato, the transcendent Forms were the eternal Truth of the universal Mind. True knowledge was attained through the direct apprehension of these transcendent Forms and not through the empirical, sensorial, temporal, corporeal, material realm of everyday phenomena. Hence, Platonic thought made a distinction – yet not a separation – of the transcendent absolute quality beyond the appearance of transiency. This has encouraged many Western scholars to interpret Plato as positing the transcendent as superior to (more enlightened than) the immanent divinity within Nature. The 'Being' of Plato's transcendent unchanging Truth has been perceived as primary to the 'Becoming' of the tangible realm of existence. Yet Plato understood the great step in wisdom as a shift in attending; from surmising about things to real knowledge of things, our knowing of being and becoming. He specified that it was through the human soul that attunement with the divine happened, and he recognised the importance of imagination, intuition and empirical, as well as rational, logic for this attainment. For Plato there is only one world (*phusis*) that includes all things.

Plato took inspiration from the Pythagoreans who were still influential amongst elites in Hellenistic Greece at that time. Pythagoras held that divine illumination was the true purpose of philosophy, and that Nature was imbued with the unfolding patterns and processes of the Divine, hence the importance of both transcendent logic through mathematical and musical order and the immanent divinity of the flowing vibrations of this mathematical and musical order embodied within Nature. It was by attuning with Nature's immanent and transcendent logic that resonance with the Divine, and so illumination, could be realised. At their heart, both Pythagoras's and Plato's teachings are essentially transformation-based in that they both view consciousness as immanent and transcendent in much the same way that ancient mystic and shamanic traditions perceive transformation of the soul within an all-pervasive World Soul, divine intelligence or Spirit. The Eternal is within *phusis* or Nature. While many scholars point to Plato prioritising the transcendent Eternal over the immanence of Nature, the modern day thinker Ken Wilber argues that Plato did not intend the transcendent aspect to devalue the immanence within the material world. And yet a degree of differentiation was made between the divine intellectual potential of the human and the rest of Nature.

Aristotle

Aristotle joined Plato's Academy at the age of eighteen. He built upon much of Plato's thinking yet disagreed with some aspects. For Aristotle, that which could be experienced in this world – the tangible rather than the intangible transcendent Forms – could be proven as fact. He rejected Plato's Forms only in the sense that the Idea or Form of a thing did not exist outside or separately from the thing or its 'matter'. Aristotle held that matter and form can only be separated *conceptually,* just as the inside and outside of a cup can only be separated conceptually, while in actuality they coexist as one. He recognised that, since it is the nature of all things to flourish, everything is 'underway' towards fruition. He understood the process of things 'becoming' in the natural world as the expression of their 'being' fulfilled through the potentiality of their form. Every form has a potentiality to it, for instance an acorn having the potentiality to become a mature oak tree. The oak tree and the acorn are one 'being-at-work', so the acorn and the oak tree are its 'nature'. Take away the coming-to-be and both the acorn and the tree vanish. So the 'potential' of things is not merely a latent possibility in them, but their power to be what they are, out of their own nature. Western philosophy scholar Joseph Milne notes that the 'beingness' (*ousia*) of things has largely disappeared from modern thought and, along with it, Aristotle's metaphysics is profoundly distorted.

Aristotle's work has been hugely influential, as philosophy historian Richard Tarnas notes:

So considerable was his encyclopaedic system of thought that most scientific activity in the West until the seventeenth century was carried out on the basis of his fourth-century BC writing, and even when moving beyond him modern science would continue his orientation and use his conceptual tools.[11]

As well as defining qualities and quantities throughout the natural order of the empirical world, he defined time as a numbered sequence of moments, a series of points that divide the now from the past and the future. The flow of 'becoming' evident in Nature could be divided up and defined with rational logic. Around 300 BC, soon after Aristotle defined time, the Greek philosopher Euclid defined space in terms of point positions and measurable geometric shapes. This was a ground-breaking perception radically different from the animism of the ancients who viewed space and time, in fact all of Nature as cycling, spiralling, interwoven relations. Thanks to Aristotle and Euclid, both time and space could be defined in a linear way. The moments and movement of life could be grasped by our rational mind.

To summarise, Plato and Aristotle, and to greater extent the Pre-socratics, implied a direct participation or participatory conscious embodiment of the divine Mind. Yet a differentiation of Nature's immanence and Spirit's transcendence emerged as did an increased reliance on rational logic. Many scholars have positioned Plato and Aristotle at the threshold of Western philosophical thought where before them Pre-socratic philosophy was deeply embedded in participation with Nature and after them a drawing away from an immersed embodiment of Nature comes with a rising emphasis on rational logic. Certainly, Platonic and Aristotelian thinking emphasises rational logic as a tool for exploring wisdom. Yet both Plato and Aristotle viewed Truth as accessible through the soul as a divine participation. To this end, rational logic was a method of analysis to aid understanding, and yet a prioritisation of the eternal from the phenomenological occurs, and this, as McGilchrist points out 'leaves an indelible stamp on the history of Western philosophy for the subsequent two thousand years.'[12]

Neo-Platonism

Teachings from Plato and early Platonists such as Plotinus, Porphyry and later Proclus combined cosmological aspects of Platonic thought with ancient mysticism and astrology to form Neo-Platonism as a school of thought which greatly influenced Christian and Islamic theology. The most notable contributions came in the third century AD from Plotinus who is regarded as the father of Neo-Platonism. Drawing on Persian and Egyptian mysticism, astrology, Judaic religion, Greek mythology, the Pre-socratics and the work of Plato and Aristotle, he formulated a philosophy based on three principles: the One, the Intellect and the Soul.[13] The transcendent One permeates all of creation and beyond. Any manifestation into the corporeal, material realm contains the essence of the One in its incorporeal soul yet becomes 'less perfect' and so deficiency is introduced. The transcendent 'potential' flows from the One through all stages of lesser perfection. This potential is not just an intellectual concept but something to be experienced; through experience one can transcend multiplicity of form and become true with the One. It is through Beauty and Good that we experience the One in this corporeal realm. The true essence of the human is the incorporeal soul and is attained through reason and contemplation.[14]

Plotinus' view of the One was of a divinity that included all multiplicity. He viewed the One as emanating of Nous (the universal Mind, Logos or reason within all universal forms) and World Soul (soul within and permeating throughout all material forms of creation) – concepts he developed from the thinking of Plato and Aristotle. This all-encompassing view of the One gives rise to what some theologians have referred to as a 'di-polar' One being both transcendent (a 'vertical pole' of the spiritual realm of universal Mind) and immanent (a 'horizontal pole' of soul within and throughout all of Creation). Plotinus' World Soul flowed through all aspects of the natural world and so cared for each and every aspect of Creation.[15] *Zoe* – the Greek for eternal life or the infinite – was the 'time of the soul' which moves from one *bios* – the Greek for finite, mortal life – to another through death and rebirth. What one finds in the Greek philosophers and Neo-Platonists is a quest for harmony between the different aspects of the soul, an attunement of the physical and the psyche, the immanent and the transcendent, the finite and the infinite.

Above and below

All major religions dedicate philosophical thought to the relation of immanence and transcendence (an exploration of which is beyond the scope of this book). What is of relevance here is a historic tendency within Western philosophy to view the spiritual realm as 'upper' and the material realm as 'lower' and so encouraging a sense of superiority of transcendent Spirit over immanent Nature. In the West, interpretative emphasis on ancient mystical texts and biblical scriptures has tended towards the One or God being viewed as essentially transcendent 'above' the material realm 'below'. This encourages a de-emphasis of the divine immanence permeating throughout Nature. Humans, time and again, have been viewed as the bridge between the 'imperfect' corporeal material realm 'below' and the transcendent universal Mind 'above'.

Christian theology

While the Greek and Roman empires helped spread Hellenistic philosophy across Western Europe, in turn influencing indigenous Western European cultures (Germanic, Gallic, Celtic, and others), it largely remained limited to the ruling classes due to a reliance on intellectual, rational debate. In contrast, Christianity penetrated deep into all levels of society due to its accessibility and universality. Regardless of education or wealth, one could become a Christian. The message of Jesus Christ was not of intellectual debate but a simple one of love and compassion.

Until the middle of the third century AD Christianity remained a cult with many Christians suffering persecution. Yet as the Roman Empire came under continual invasion the personal courage, conviction and compassion of the early Christians impressed others in such times of turmoil. Increasingly Christianity presented itself as a worldview whose time had come and soon its take-up culminated in the Roman emperor Constantine converting to Christianity while experiencing a vision during battle. Christianity was no longer a sect but accepted and then disseminated by the Roman Empire as far as Ethiopia, Arabia and throughout the West. As Christianity gained popularity, philosophical schools of thought blended with Christian theology. Western Christianity as a theological philosophy drew both from Hebrew morality and Hellenistic logic. [16]

In the late fourth century, St Augustine's writings greatly influenced Christian philosophy and while he developed his own blend of theological philosophy, his thinking was influenced by Stoicism, Neo-Platonism, Gnosticism, Judaic monotheism and ancient mysticism. Augustine's work helped unify Christianity at a time of much fracturing and sect forming. His views founded the Catholic Church and projected an innate paradox: humans were sinful and tainted with evil (Original Sin emanating from the Fall of Adam and Eve) and yet could lead good Christian lives and so gain salvation. Augustine's Fall was an alienation of humanity from Truth and contained a strong Platonic element, where the soul has forgotten its origin in the divine world and yearns to return home. While Augustine recognised the sacredness of Nature and the humble holiness of all things, his doctrine encouraged an alienation of humanity from Nature and seemed to undermine the participatory embodiment of human life immersed within the divine immanence of Nature. As the political historian Jack Holland notes:

> At the centre of the turmoil of Augustine's search for God is the struggle between the desire of the flesh and striving of the will, the profound dualism that Augustine will incorporate into the very heart of Catholicism using Plato's philosophical apparatus.[17]

Christianity, which originally set out to spread Jesus Christ's teachings of transcendent and immanent love and compassion flowing through all relations within all things, became God-fearing with limited free will to prevent perishing upon Judgement Day. And yet this doctrine of eternal salvation, unlike the educational elitism of Western philosophy up to this point, was inclusive for all people and the Catholic Church managed to survived the collapse of the Roman Empire in the fifth century to establish Western Christendom with an ecclesiastical network spanning the continent and operating alongside a variety of European monarchies and clans. The main aim of Christianity then became converting pagan non-believers – whose belief, by and large, was of participating within the transcendent and immanent animating spirit of Nature. Most belief-systems practised before and during early Christianity (such as Egyptian, Persian and Celtic) viewed their gods as interwoven with the natural world with humanity embodied within Nature.[18] In contrast, Christianity focused on the Judaeo-Christian notion that God created humanity in His image with dominion over the rest of Creation. While the Hebrew biblical narrative talks of the reciprocal nature of immanence and transcendence, over time the immanent aspect of God permeating throughout Nature became de-emphasised and the transcendent aspect of God emphasised (we explore the origins of this trend in the next chapter). Mythologist Joseph Campbell has noted that:

> ... the Christian separation of matter and spirit, of the dynamism of life and the realm of the spirit, of natural grace and supernatural grace, has really castrated nature. And the European mind, the European life, has been, as it were, emasculated by this separation.[19]

Immanent divinity within Nature was not to be altogether excluded from Christian theology, even if it was viewed as secondary to the transcendent aspect. For instance, later in the ninth century, Johannes Scotus Eriugena – better known as 'John the Scot' even though he was actually an Irish scholar – revived philosophical thought in Western Europe re-introducing Neo-Platonism into the scholasticism of Medieval European monastic schools leading to its increased influence on Christian theology. His famous philosophical work *The Division of Nature* details his views on the hierarchical structure of Nature as God's Creation.[20] In the eleventh and twelfth centuries Nature was regarded as the 'second book' of revelation, after the Scriptures. And at the turn of the twelfth and thirteenth century St Francis of Assisi preached that all creatures were part of God's kingdom with humanity's duty being the stewardship of God's creation. Both John the Scot and Francis of Assisi understood God and his creation as one of the same allowing for a re-embracing of the divine immanence flowing throughout Nature, a re-sacralisation of Nature within Christian theology. In referring to the Gospel of John 14:2, 'all things are from Him, through Him, and directed towards Him', John the Scot stated that there is divinity of being within matter itself.[21] This view was seen as heretical by the

Church as seen as placing God within an 'impure' natural world and so his work was condemned by the Church. Yet later in the thirteenth century, Thomas Aquinas greatly influenced Christian theological philosophy. For Aquinas, all things exist fully in the Mind of God, and without their existence as a participation in God's existence they would have no existence at all. He took Aristotle's natural order of things and situated Nature within Grace.

To summarise, medieval Christian doctrine tended towards prioritising the transcendent realm over the immanence of Nature and largely viewed humanity as superior to and separate from the natural world. Yet there have been notable influential exceptions such as Aquinas, John the Scot, Francis of Assisi, and not in the least Jesus Christ himself who said, 'Cleave a wood, I am there; lift up the stone and you will find me there.'[22]

The Renaissance

The Renaissance (meaning 'rebirth') was a cultural era that commenced in Italy in the fourteenth century and spread throughout the West into the seventeenth century. It spawned revolutionary and innovative philosophical views challenging the dominant Christian orthodoxy. Great minds like Leonardo Da Vinci, Nicolaus Copernicus, Franceso Patrizi, Giordano Bruno and Tommaso Campanella revisited ancient animist, mystical and Pre-socratic perspectives of the world as well as Platonic, Aristotelian, Neo-Platonic and Christian perspectives. For instance, Bruno viewed all forms as animated by a World Soul. He felt that the imagination, if trained through visualisation and contemplative exercises, could assist personal transformation towards inner harmony and greater outer attunement with the world, enabling a cosmic connection with the rhythms of the universe.[23] The emphasis on a transformative path to achieve divine purity through meditation and imaginative expressions such as dancing or chanting had origins in the ancient Greek mysticism of Orpheus which itself was influenced by mystic alchemic practices from further afield as well as the shamanic practices of Neolithic Europe. Unfortunately his visionary views were seen as heretical by the Church and led to him being burned alive.

Another great mind of the Renaissance was Campanella who

combined both the experiential with the conceptual to form a comprehensive philosophical system. He viewed all matter to be sensory and all living beings as sentient. For Campanella all things participate in reality with love and are part of God. He said, 'if animals are sentient ... the elements whereby they and everything else are brought into being must be said to be sentient.'[24] While Campanella joined the Church's Dominican Order at the age of fifteen, his views on the divinity of animist Nature led to him being cited before the Church, confined to a convent for a number of years and then later tortured and imprisoned whereupon he feigned madness to avoid death.

The Renaissance helped revive some of the belief in Nature's sacredness, and yet by the close of the Middle Ages, the eternal omnipotent Will of God became distant from His ever-changing Creation. Puritanism formed by the theologies of Luther and Calvin and the Church Reformation (c.1517–1648) helped create dualism within our minds, bodies and psyches; the full implications of this manifest in the Scientific Revolution and permeate modernity from Descartes to the present day.

The shift from medieval to modernity

During the Middle Ages the Christian theological philosophers, known as the Scholastics, modified Aristotelian thought into what became referred to as 'medieval Aristotle'. This medieval Aristotle applied increasing emphasis on the mathematical approach to philosophy, viewing mathematical propositions as the foundation of reason.[25] Descartes received much of his philosophical teaching from a Jesuit scholastic school in La Flèche, France. Descartes later went on to radicalise the mathematical laws whereby abstract mathematical propositions became the ground from which his objectifying approach grew. Newton and others then utilised this approach, and we find abstract mathematical propositions underpinning Newton's Laws of Motion along with much of Western science from then on. This radicalisation of the mathematical may have gained inspiration from Aristotle yet it is substantially different from his original thinking. No longer is there an intuitive, empathic and embodied understanding of Nature.

Modernity is an abstract rationalisation of reality within the 'I' realm of 'pure reason'. Political philosopher Leo Strauss notes that:

… knowledge is no longer understood as fundamentally receptive; the initiative in understanding is with man, not with the cosmic order, in seeking knowledge man calls nature before the tribunal of his reason … The purpose of science is reinterpreted; *propter potentiam,* for the relief of man's estate, for the conquest of nature for the maximum control, the systemic control of the natural conditions of human life.[26]

And so this shift towards modernity comes with a severing of natural law and human affairs. Nature is reduced to an artefact of civilisation and human politics. Objectified Nature is to be tested, analysed, atomised and controlled for the self-preservation of humanity which comes to be viewed in some way as separate from, rather than embodied within, Nature. The sacred and animate purposefulness of Nature is no longer. In contrast, Aristotle viewed the imitation of Nature as the purposeful activity of philosophy; this imitation of Nature involved the receptive, intuitive, soulful, metaphorical, empirical, rational, imaginal and contemplative ways of knowing. For Aristotle, 'the forms in the world give man the concepts to contemplate.'[27] As the modern day philosopher Jeremy Naydler puts it, 'For Aristotle nature is the outpouring of spirit, which is the active or creative principle in all things.'[28] Yet with modernity's prioritisation of abstract rationality, this imitation of Nature debases into little more than super-imposed copying of functional forms, structures and compositions for human utility; content is extracted from its deeper context which is largely overlooked by the narrowly-focused lens of rationalism.

To summarise, while differentiations developed through Platonic and Aristotelian thought, the Pre-socratics, Plato, Aristotle and the Neo-Platonists viewed humanity and Nature as inseparably participating within the World Soul. Yet by the time of Descartes, the shamanic mystical immersions of the Pre-socratics was quite removed from Western philosophy with its tendency towards abstract rationality and intellectualised thought coupled with a sense of separation from a de-sacralised world. In the next chapter we go further upstream to explore the formation of Western civilisation.

5. The Fall

The image of opposition – of the heroic consciousness banishing chaos to create and order the world – became the model for the way of thinking by which civilization was sustained.

Anne Baring and Jules Cashford[1]

Our modern day understanding of human evolution is based on fragmented fossil findings dated over a long duration with new discoveries giving fresh insight all the while. *Homo sapiens* (meaning 'wise man' in Latin) are thought to have emigrated from sub-Sahara Africa around 100,000 years ago, then spreading throughout the world: Australia around 50,000 years ago; the Pacific Islands around 33,000 years ago; the Americas around 15,000 years ago. By 12,000 years ago the Ice Age was drawing to a close with vegetation and animals spread across northern regions of Europe and Asia; humans numbering a few million. Around 10,000 years ago the Neolithic agricultural revolution commenced with the formation of permanent settlements and agricultural farming. A huge cultural shift took place as more and more foragers began to settle in sites all year round. Population increased as did the dependency on agriculture as settlements became more complex.[2] Four widely dispersed, socially complex civilisations emerged apparently independently around 8-6,000 BC: the lower Tigris and Euphrates valleys; the valley of the Nile; the Indus valley and around Harrappa and Mohenjo-Daro; and the Yellow River around Anyang. The modern words 'civilised' and 'civilisation' come from the Latin *civilis,* meaning orderly. *Civilis* originates from an older Latin word *civis* meaning 'someone who lives in a city', a citizen.[3] The characteristic feature of all of these early civilisations was the formation of large urbanised centres – cities – as a dominant social form, along with division of labour, literacy and political and military hierarchies.[4] Urbanisation came with the instilling of human structure, routine and control. Nature needed to be domesticated on an increasingly larger scale in order to serve urban life. This transformed the relationship of people and Nature, while also transforming communal relations between people.

Animism

Before the Neolithic agricultural revolutions, and the subsequent formations of urbanised civilisations, all of humanity was in every day contact with wildlife. In order to survive and thrive, humans learned how to engage with everything around them, viewing and sensing the interplay of life in its raw abundance. Back then, all humans were immersed in, and felt a deep empathy with, their natural neighbourhood.[5] This deep empathy is the essence of animism which, for the vast majority of human history, was how we related to, and experienced, the world. Graham Harvey, the author of the book *Animism,* views animism as a way of engaging self with human and non-human others: 'Animism is the attempt to live respectfully as members of the diverse community of living persons (only some of whom are human) which we call the world or cosmos.'[6] As far as we can tell from historic records, all ancient cultures have animist roots. Ancient cultures held the belief that Nature was sacred, full of spirit flowing with divinity; nothing was perceived as inert matter, not even mountains or rocks, for instance, which flow with their own spirit and aliveness. When speaking of the animism of the Etruscans of ancient Italy D.H. Lawrence said:

> To the Etruscan all was alive, the whole universe lived ... and had a great soul, or *anima:* and in spite of one great soul, there were myriad roving, lesser souls; every man, every creature and tree and lake and mountain and stream, was animate, and had its own peculiar consciousness.[7]

These animist cultures are essentially shamanic. Shamanism is deep attunement with Nature; it is animism's belief system or practice. In studying different shamanic cultures, the anthropologist Michael Harner, author of *The Way of The Shaman,* realised that there was a remarkable consistency of thought, beliefs and practices between animist cultures worldwide. He coined the phrase 'core shamanism' for these common practices.[8] Our ancestors used to shape these core shamanic practices to the times and environment in which they lived. These practices instilled a deep sense of empathy for other human and non-human beings and the environment as an ensemble.

Here are some basic principles of core shamanism:

1. Everything is made of energy (spirit).
2. This energy/spirit is alive and conscious.
3. Everything is therefore alive and conscious.
4. Everything and all human beings are included in a living flow of energy.
5. Everything is conscious and within communicative reach (this can be done through what is known as 'shamanic journeying' using deep awareness and intention).
6. When we communicate with things, we understand them and feel empathy with them.
7. Thus, shamanic practices bring a deep, heart-felt empathy with, and reverence for, all things.
8. This helps us live in harmony and 'right relationship' with each other as people and the environment, and engage in 'right action'.
9. Human beings have the (seemingly unique) ability to 'unplug' themselves from the flow.
10. This unplugs us from this sense of empathy and 'right relationship', and we no longer act with 'right action'.
11. This makes us ill individually, as organisations and as societies (physically, mentally, emotionally and spiritually), and leads to us harming others and the environment.
12. In unplugging and separating off we lose something profound. This is known as 'soul loss'.
13. Healthy human beings (and so, healthy human organisations and societies) feel included within Nature, not separate from it or superior to it. [9]

In his book *The Fall*, Steve Taylor shows that, far from living brutish lives, these ancient animist cultures tended to live quite peacefully, with excellent mental health, functioning cooperatively and sustainably.[10] For Taylor, when we lost our shamanism we lost our way; we lost our empathy and mutual engagement with life.[11] In the words of holistic scientist Stephan Harding: '[we] are beginning to realise that animistic peoples, far from being 'primitive', have been living a reality which holds many important insights for our own relationships with each other and with the Earth.'[12]

Why civilisation?

There are many theories about how civilisation came about and just because there is little evidence today of civilised life before 10,000 years ago, this does not necessarily mean that in the long interval between 100,000 and 10,000 years ago nothing but hunter-gatherer, semi-nomadic, 'uncivilised' communities of *Homo sapiens* walked the Earth. The fragments of evidence we have seem to point to hunter-gatherers forming into settled agriculturalist and semi-nomadic pastoralist ways of living during the Neolithic revolution. Like the agriculturalists, the pastoralists did domesticate animals and plants yet travelled throughout different terrains with their herds, while grazing, hunting and gathering as they travelled. These pastoralists seem to have coexisted and in many cases had a symbiotic relationship with the settled agriculturalists.[13]

Around the time of the Neolithic revolution, there is evidence of a rapid climate shift with large scale desertification in Asia and North Africa along with more frequent droughts and floods which must have put pressure on food sources for both the settled and semi-nomadic communities. One theory suggests that irrigation started to be used extensively as the climate became drier. According to this theory, irrigation systems became so complex and time-consuming that central authority was required – though it is uncertain whether the complex irrigation systems came about because of civilisation rather than its cause. Some think that increasing population came about because of a settled way of life which then put pressure on resources when climate conditions rapidly changed. Yet there is evidence of civilisations forming without increases in population. In Sumer, for instance, it seems the population may have actually been declining around the time when civilisation is thought to have begun.[14]

Another theory is that during the period of time when settled agriculturalists and semi-nomadic pastoralists lived alongside each other, the rapid environmental change and subsequent scarcity of resources encouraged the pastoralists to expropriate resources from settled communities. The more aggressive the tribe the better they fared by encroaching on and stealing food sources from settled communities, which in turn meant the settled communities had to defend themselves more readily and often. Scientist Rupert Sheldrake surmises, in his book *The Rebirth of Nature,* that the semi-nomadic pastoralists could easily transform themselves into aggressive warriors focused on dominating other people in times of strife as they were practised in hunting as well as dominating large herds of animals.[15] Interestingly, there seems to have been a difference in culture and mythology forming between the pastoralists and the agriculturalists around this time. It seems the pastoralists were more patriarchal, valued masculine force and bravery and worshipped sky-gods.[16] Whereas the agriculturalists tended to be more equalitarian (equally valuing the contribution of men and women in society), both sky-gods and earth-goddesses were worshipped, with peaceful community life valued more than bravery and force.

Another theory is what Steve Taylor calls an 'Ego Explosion'. The transforming environment helped transform the psyche of the people. A new kind of intelligence developed – a more competitive, self-centred, analytical way of viewing the world. The philosopher Ken Wilber and others have explored this new type of thinking which emerged, viewing it as sharpened, more focused, with an increased sense of self-reflection and rationality.[17] This Ego Explosion self-perpetuated its own dominance as a cultural way of attending. As we became more 'in our heads' (or as McGilchrist might say 'in our left brain hemispheres') for analytical planning, domestication and organising military offensives, our heartfelt empathic relation with the natural world weakened along with our innate primal awareness of Nature. We had to make up for our reduced embodied awareness of the natural world through increased exploitation of natural resources and each other, and so more analytical planning was required to effect such exploitation. The more aggressive and analytical the culture became the more aggressive and analytical it had to become. The environmental shift had led to a cultural shift which then became, largely self-fulfilling. Interestingly, the rise of patriarchy seems to couple with this Ego Explosion, and perhaps they came about because of each other. It is difficult to define specifics here and any conjectural theory has its flaws, yet the rise of patriarchy (and its effect on the ego, and vice versa) clearly had a profound effect on the culture of the West regardless of the specific original causations.

Patriarchy in the West

From evidence it seems that Palaeolithic and Neolithic communities throughout Europe, in the main, were neither patriarchal nor matriarchal but equalitarian where both women and men influenced all aspects of society and where social stratification was the exception rather than the rule. Societies were predominantly peaceful with shared or common ownership, referred to as 'partnership' societies by cultural scholar Riane Eisler in *The Chalice and the Blade*.[18] In *The Myth of The Goddess*, mythology historians Anne Baring and Jules Cashford point out that:

> Our assumptions about human nature, in particular our beliefs about the capacity of human beings to live in harmony with the rest of nature and to shape a peaceful world, are crucial to whether or not we can actually create a better way of being. If we hold that human beings are and always have been primarily hunters and warriors, then we are more likely to overlook evidence to the contrary and conclude that war-like aggression is innate. No evidence has been found that Palaeolithic people fought each other.[19]

Further afield in North Africa, Central Asia and the Indus valley, patriarchal societies started to dominate perhaps due to the concoction of rapid climate change, Ego Explosion and increasing aggression. These societies are referred to as 'dominator' societies by Eisler. From as early as 4,300 BC waves of invasions came into Europe from the Steppes, the Urals, the Middle East and North Africa. The invaders were diverse in their cultures yet all shared a dominator model of society – patriarchal, hierarchic and violent – in stark contrast to the partnership model of the indigenous European cultures. Technologies tended to be developed largely for destructive purposes with the primary way of gaining material wealth being through war and oppression. Society was elitist with social stratification based on private ownership of property along with male domination over women and other men, including slavery.[20] With each wave of invasion, further waves of cultural transformation occurred. The Achaean invaders of Mycenaean times and the Dorian invaders who displaced them each absorbed aspects of the culture of the peoples they conquered.[21] Social equality became a thing of the past as social inequality became the cultural norm. This patriarchal, hierarchic, elitist culture was prevalent throughout Europe by 2,000 BC, the notable exception being the Minoan culture. The Minoan culture on the island of ancient Crete seemed to remain largely equalitarian until *circa* 1,400 BC. It was a sophisticated culture with women taking active roles in all aspects of society and succession passed through the female line.[22] Some view the legend of Atlantis as referring to the Minoan culture, a lost world where people had a deep understanding of the cosmic forces at play in Nature.[23]

It is worth noting that the indigenous cultures of Neolithic Europe seemed to be creative and inventive, developing technologies for growing food, construction, clothing and manufacturing as well as social practices such as story-telling, dance, drama, music and art along with animal and plant domestication and the formulation of governance and law systems. And so European culture was not necessarily improved by the arrival of invaders whose technology was predominantly focused on aggression and oppression useful for the formation of empires built on exploitation and control. And yet while the indigenous equalitarianism influenced Hellenistic Greece, it was the patriarchal dominator model of the invaders that would most significantly influence its culture and philosophy, leading to a widening in the relation of humans and Nature and a delineation between domesticated, urbanised civilisation and 'uncivilised' wildness.

The sacred feminine

The term 'Goddess' or 'Great Mother' refers to the ancient conceptualisation of the powers governing the universe, with related images found throughout Europe dating back as far as 20,000 years ago. Cave paintings and sculptures symbolise the Goddess as being central to worship. As Pythagoras noted, anthropomorphic representations of the Goddess have been depicted over millennia through projections of the various stages of the life of the female, such as with the young maid, the mature woman and the old grandmother.[24] The word 'nature' derives from the Latin word *natura* which means 'birth', harking back to a time when the Great Mother was viewed as the source and nurturer of Nature. The Goddess holds the transformative power of birth and death; the mystery of the un-manifest becoming manifest, being created through the cosmic womb as a transformer of life. Baring and Cashford explore the image of the Goddess in the West through the lenses of archaeology, anthropology, mythology and archetypal psychology and note, 'Darkness was not something antagonistic to light, nor death to life, but an aspect of the being of the Mother Goddess.'[25] Life and death, in this mythological expression of primordial experience, were not perceived as opposites but rather as phases of the endless cyclic rhythms of Nature, much like the moon's phases continually progress through darkness and light and back again in a way that influences the pulsating rhythms of life on Earth. Hence in Neolithic mythology, lunar notations, the serpentine path, the spiral, the snake, the egg, the pregnant female and symbols of metamorphosis are all images of the sacred immanence within Nature and the regenerative quality of life. As Eisler points out:

> Both mythical and archaeological evidence indicate that perhaps the most notable quality of the pre-dominator mind was its recognition of our oneness with all of nature, which lies at the heart of both the Neolithic and the Cretan worship of the Goddess.[26]

Neolithic art is notable not just for its depiction of the sacred feminine but also for its absence of imagery of male-centred violence or conquests which frequent the art of the Western civilisation that followed.[27]

God divorced from Goddess

In early Babylonian mythology the goddess Tiamat is the dark, oceanic, cosmic womb which birthed the world. The god Marduk – the creator – was her son. From around 2,000 BC onwards, in this Babylonian mythology the goddess became a chaotic force of Nature to be mastered, and the god became a remote, transcendent creator.[28] Marduk went on to destroy his mother and in so doing creating the firmament of Heaven and Earth.[29] Transcendence (Heaven) was perceived as above the immanence of Nature (Earth). The Judaic religion inherited aspects of this Babylonian mythology that encouraged a separation between Spirit and Nature.[30] The transcendent Father God (Yahweh) as pure Spirit imbued creation with its animating potential – the Word. In the book of Genesis, the primal Mother was a dark, watery abyss, and God then divided the light from the dark, waters below, Heaven from Earth. For Baring and Cashford, this separation of light from dark, of transcendent Spirit from immanent Nature, came with a growing sense of self as separate from the natural world and each other.[31] It is worth noting that the Judaic mysticism of Kabbalah contains the understanding of the divine immanence of Nature through the sacred feminine aspect of the Godhead, Shekinah, yet this aspect is largely obscured from mainstream Judaic, Islamic and Christian religions today.

Catalysts for this polarisation of immanence and transcendence could have been: Steve Taylor's Ego Explosion hypothesis, where a more egotistic way of attending perceives self as separate from Nature; increasing patriarchal aggression in turn repression of the Feminine; increasing domestication in turn repression of wild Nature; increasing urbanisation as part-and-parcel of the civilising process weakening our embodied relation with Nature. Perhaps a mix of these factors contributed to the cultural, mythological, psychical and philosophical shift that ensured Western civilisation would be influenced by a dominator model of separateness: masculine from feminine, transcendent from immanent, human from Nature.

6. The Evolution of Western Ways of Attending

The intuitive mind is a sacred gift and the rational mind is a faithful servant. We have created a society that honours the servant and has forgotten the gift.

Albert Einstein[1]

In concluding Part One, we summarise here three important explorations into the evolution of our Western ways of attending: primary and final participation by Owen Barfield, the left and right-brain hemispheres by Iain McGilchrist, and the Ego Explosion by Steve Taylor. Each of these explorations do not promise a definitive explanation, if there were such a thing, for such a rich and far-reaching topic, and of course there are many more than these three, yet in summarising these we get a good flavour of the historic trend in our Western ways of attending to help us formulate our own perspectives before we move on to Part Two.

From original participation to final participation

In his profound book, *Saving the Appearances*, British philosopher Owen Barfield explores what he calls *original participation*, *separation* (*alpha* and *beta thinking*), and *final participation* (see Figure 6.1). *Original participation* is the primary sensory and embodied experience of the phenomenon, then *alpha thinking* is where we rationalise, objectify and define what we experience and so abstract it from its lived-in context. *Beta thinking* then reflects on this alpha understanding bringing in memory of past experiences along with future expectations. *Final participation* is when, after engaging in *alpha* and *beta* extrapolations of our *original participation* we then recontextualise our conscious understanding within its lived-in participatory dynamic of reality.

Original participation – (Animism)

↘

   Alpha and beta thinking – (Aristotelian thought
   culminating in detached Cartesian thinking)

   ↘

      Final participation – (Imaginative, intuitive, poetic
      perception of an unfolding co-creative participation)

Figure 6.1: Barfield's Shift from Original Participation to Final Participation

For Barfield, it is systemic alpha thinking that brings our rational mind to the fore, which can – if allowed to become the dominant mode of perception – undermine the participative experiential dialogue or felt-relation of original participation and so skew our experience of reality. According to Barfield, systemic alpha thinking began with Western philosophy and its focus on astronomy as the great Greek minds interested themselves in regularity and predictability as a source of eternal truth.[2] Barfield notes that Plato and Aristotle increasingly relied upon alpha thinking in their quest for truth.

While recognising the difficulty of identifying an inflection point where alpha thinking became dominant in the West, Barfield views the shift from Platonic to Aristotelian thinking as a pivotal time. He notes that:

Although Aristotle was the pupil of Plato, there are many good reasons for treating the former as beginning a new epoch, and the latter as closing an old one, while not forgetting that all such exact limitations of period have about them something artificial and arbitrary. At some point a thing ceases to be a flower and becomes a fruit; but who shall say exactly when? In Raphael's fresco of the School of Athens in the Vatican, the two figures of Plato and Aristotle stand side by side, the one with raised hand pointing upwards to the heavens, the other pointing earthward down a flight of steps. If, in imagination, we take our stand between the two, we can indeed look forward, through the thinking which found expression in Aristotle, to the collective representations of the Western world which were to take their course, through the so-called dark and middle ages, down to the scientific revolution and beyond. While through the other, through the star-and-space-involved thinking of Plato, we may peer backward into the collective representations of the East and of the past.[3]

Barfield explores a diminution of participatory consciousness as a shift in the perception of phenomena flowing within a participatory flux into a perspective of phenomena as discrete things: objectification. For Barfield, both the ancient Greeks and the ancient Jews contributed to the diminution of participatory consciousness: the Greeks through increasing focus on the phenomenon for its own sake, and the Jews for a quite different reason, in their focus on Yahweh as Creator divorced from his Creation, with the Word to be uttered by humankind who was made in His image. Yet, this Word has a participating aspect in its unfolding of God's wisdom, albeit with an emphasis on the transcendent God rather than an immanent flux of divinity. Barfield notes that the Word of Judaic-Christian theology had both inner and outer consciousness and was quite different from the abstraction of external phenomena within aspects of Greco-Roman philosophy. Yet by the time Jesus was born the Divine Name had become objectified into a remote superior being, divorced from Creation.[4] Jesus spoke of Christ as present within each of us and throughout Creation. These teachings assisted in bridging the gulf between God, humankind and Nature. Also the alpha thinking of rationalistic empiricism blended with mystical pagan consciousness and Judaic patriarchal theology. And participatory consciousness lived alongside alpha thinking.

For Barfield, the Scientific Revolution marked a crucial stage in the West's evolution of consciousness; the transformation into what Barfield calls 'modern consciousness' where alpha thinking became supreme. Original participation was largely suppressed into the unconscious myth. Barfield notes, 'Space, as a mindless, wisdomless, lifeless void, was not a common notion at any time before the scientific revolution.'[5] Alpha thinking's abstract re-presentations of reality became more than just a tool or mechanism for exploring the nature of reality. Science begun to believe its own abstractions were the ultimate, absolute Truth.[6] Hence the hypothetical model of rationalism became the new religion; no longer was a 'mover' or psyche or World Soul or divine Mind required as all could be explained through the mechanism of science. As Francis Bacon and other great minds of the Enlightenment understood, with science humankind could gain power and control over Nature which became nothing more than a collection of things to objectify and define through abstract rational logic and empirical experimentation. The transformation from our animist original participation to alpha and beta thinking had been made complete with the Scientific Revolution. Our way of perceiving was no longer participatory but linear, atomised, materialistic. It is as if the razor-sharp gaze of our 'rational eye' drained the life-blood out of the World Soul, leaving a collection of things to be manipulated for soulless material betterment.

As we saw in Chapter 2, Darwinism, and subsequently Neo-Darwinism, came of age in this climate of alpha thinking where collective representations posited as fact became collective beliefs influencing all scientific explorations – a vicious cycle of abstract analysis fuelling further abstract analysis. The organism was viewed as separate from its lived-in context and biological evolution became viewed as a purely random, competitive affair. Any embedded meaning within Nature was abstracted away to leave the building blocks of nothing more than selfish genes. The classical and medieval doctrine that all things in Nature are moved by a 'mover' was at last abandoned and a complete separation of the spiritual dimension from the physical world formed. Barfield notes:

The plain fact is, that all the unity and coherence of nature depends on participation of one kind or the other. If therefore man succeeds in eliminating all original participation, without substituting any other, he will have done nothing less than eliminate all meaning and all coherence from the cosmos.[7]

For Barfield, it is this alpha and beta thinking, this analysis of content from context, that allows for the further evolution of consciousness towards 'final participation'. Our self and collective perception of the participatory nature of reality becomes fully conscious, as we awaken to the transcendent immanence of the divinity flowing through all of life. In final participation, focusing on phenomena in a singular, objectified way (alpha thinking) is enhanced with the deeper perspective of the unfolding 'becoming' of phenomena. Johann von Goethe and Rudolf Steiner are two Western philosophers who have helped pave the way for this evolution towards Barfield's final participation. Goethe used an 'active-passive' way of seeing to perceive the figuration, or potential becoming, of phenomena. Steiner developed Goethe's method of perceiving to investigate potentiality through imagination, inspiration and intuition to understand the wider lived-in context of phenomena. These, and the important developments within Western thinking of phenomenology and process philosophy, are prime examples of profound shifts in perception from alpha and beta thinking towards final participation – we explore these in Part Two.

The rise of left hemisphere awareness

Neuroscientist Iain McGilchrist has synthesised much of today's findings on how the brain influences our perception of reality in his masterpiece *The Master and His Emissary.* His thesis is that the left and right brain hemispheres interrelate in ways that affect not just our perception but our Western worldview.

The bi-hemispheric brain enables us to attend to the world with seemingly incompatible types of attention at the same time: a broad, open and embodied way (right hemisphere) as well as a narrow, focused and abstracted way (left hemisphere).[8] We benefit from understanding reality in its full-flow, ever-changing context as well as in its broken down, static, fragmented parts. Hence, we can rationalise our subjective understanding of reality through our ability to abstract, fix, isolate and compartmentalise and so build up our understanding in an explicit and objective way. This fragmented re-presentation of reality by the left hemisphere is fundamentally different from the world in its real life context as it lacks embodiment and inter-subjective being. How we attend – whether our attention is primarily left-brained or right-brained – changes how we perceive reality and in turn drives our beliefs, values and behaviours. As McGilchrist notes, 'Attention is a moral act: it creates, brings aspects of things into being, but in doing so makes others recede. What a thing is depends on who is attending to it and in what way.'[9] And it seems our left and right brain hemispheres provide awareness and attention in quite different ways. The right hemisphere's awareness is essentially passive and receptive, left hemisphere awareness is active and responsive. As the philosopher and writer Colin Wilson describes, 'Right brain awareness is like a broad, gently flowing stream; left brain awareness is like a powerful jet of water.'[10] The right hemisphere's attention is more of a heightened sense of presence. When we experience a new situation we can sometimes feel this heightened sense of contextual awareness. The left hemisphere's is more a focussed attention. It is the left hemisphere rather than the right that likes what it already knows and so prioritises the expected.[11] This can sometimes cause us to assume we saw or heard something familiar (like a phone ringing) whereas it was actually something new or unusual which the left hemisphere prioritised, in the moment of ambiguity, with something already known. Hence, while the right hemisphere with its freer more creative, exploratory style of attention can deal with radically different contextual situations and frame shifts, the left hemisphere grasps on to what it knows which can inhibit our acceptance of change.[12] Left hemisphere awareness often brings a sense of grasping narrowness that traps us in our heads and alienates us from our instincts, imagination, intuition and embodied experiences of the world as we focus in on the object of attention. Interestingly, the more we become aware of our narrowly focussed, change-fearing left hemisphere's attention, the more focussed our attention can become. The left hemisphere has difficulty disengaging as its manner of grasping accentuates if something is not yet understood. It is only with a relaxation of attention that the left hemisphere weakens its grasp. Perhaps we feel this sometimes when we cannot 'see the wood from the trees' yet get the urge to dive deeper into detail, analysing the problem into yet smaller component parts in the hope of getting to the bottom of it, when actually we need to step back and regain the contextual situation in order to gain better perspective.

The right hemisphere understands the dynamic relationships within context and has a capacity for empathy, whereas the left hemisphere dissects relationships into their parts and so views the world mechanistically and competitively. It is the right hemisphere that seeks the reconciliation of opposing tensions and relational differences found between phenomena. Whereas the left tends to polarise in its search for purity and rationality, in which one aspect of the tension must be selected as correct over the other, and so the other aspect is excluded, even annihilated. The right hemisphere's impulse is towards harmony, whereas the left's impulse is towards singleness.[13] This singling out by the left's rationality creates dualistic paradoxes such as human-Nature, whereas the right's empathy and perception of relational betweenness recognises the deeper reality beyond dualism. For the right hemisphere time is an undivided flow whereas the left tries to abstract time by breaking it up into units – like Aristotle did for time and Euclid did for space. While the right hemisphere is concerned with what it experiences, the left hemisphere is concerned with what it knows.[14] As a result, the left hemisphere tends to prefer man-made devices which can be mechanistically understood rather than natural, continually changing aliveness. As McGilchrist notes, 'The model of the machine is the only one that the left hemisphere likes'.[15]

McGilchrist explores how this inter-hemispheric relation works when neither is dominating the other: The right hemisphere contextualises or constitutes our experience, the left consolidates what the right hemisphere brings to attention, the right recontextualises that consolidation into renewed exploration.[16] This inter-hemispheric relationship enables our perception to enhance and transform our engagement with the world. The right hemisphere needs the left hemisphere to sift through the ever-changing flow of experience. Left hemisphere attention is vital for our analysis of reality and is what allows for a transformation in perception to occur. While complementation is needed between the left and right hemispheres, what seems like inter-hemispheric competition can and does arise. Within our mind's consciousness – what McGilchrist likens to a tree of consciousness branching out from the lower levels of the brain into the frontal lobes, much like the canopy of a forest – there can be two wills. It is the corpus callosum which integrates these wills into the 'self' although conflicts can arise when one hemisphere manages to dominate the other and so the self embodies more of the values and experiences of the dominating hemisphere. The criticality of the right-left-right inter-hemispheric relationship is that the left hemisphere plays a vital role *only* if what it has abstracted can be restored by being recontextualised by the right hemisphere. Much like Barfield's alpha thinking, left hemisphere attention forms a vital aspect of what makes us human, yet needs to be reborn into the lived-in flow of reality if we are to attend to the world in a harmonious way.

During the history of the Western world, according to McGilchrist, the left hemisphere has usurped control and far from loosening its grip it is self-perpetuating its own delusion; he notes:

> It is as though, blindly, the left hemisphere pushes on, always along the same track. Evidence of failure does not mean that we are going in the wrong direction, only that we have not gone far enough in the direction we are already headed.[17]

Rather sinisterly, the left hemisphere's grasping manner of further abstracting its abstraction in order to get to the bottom of things leads to yet more abstract artificiality with devastating consequences on how we attend to reality. Enter the individualistic techno-sphere of today's Western way of life. The qualities of the left hemisphere have enabled us to form a civilisation based on advanced technology, rationality, social stratification, manipulation and control. This way of attending gives us a sense of power and control over our world which is alluring and self-enhancing yet self-contained and ultimately dislocated from reality.

While Barfield points to Plato and Aristotle as standing on either side of the alpha thinking cusp, McGilchrist notes that Plato's Forms are disembodied abstract ideals and that Plato's thinking has a certainty and clarity, hallmarks of the left hemisphere. McGilchrist also notes that Aristotle's honouring of *phronesis* – as facilitating the wisdom of Sophia through the empirical world – is more right hemisphere than Plato's focus on abstract ideals. For McGilchrist, Plato's and Aristotle's work marked an increase in left hemisphere dominance in Greek philosophy.[18] As to the Scientific Revolution and Reformation, McGilchrist suggests that the Enlightenment's belief that Nature, fate and destiny could be controlled – or in some way 'civilised' – is essentially the outlook of the left hemisphere. He notes:

> There are obvious continuities between the Reformation and the Enlightenment. They share the same marks of left hemisphere

domination: the banishment of wonder; the triumph of the explicit, and, with it, mistrust of metaphor; alienation from the embodied world of the flesh, and a consequent cerebralisation of life and experience.[19]

McGilchrist points to both the French and American Revolutions' explicit pursuit of liberty and happiness as left hemisphere grasping, rather than the right hemisphere's fashion of allowing these qualities to emerge within the world; he says, 'The liberty of the left hemisphere is, as is bound to be the case, an abstract concept, not what experience teaches us through living.'[20] He goes on to note:

> Democracy as Jefferson saw it, with its essentially local, agrarian, communitarian, organic structure, was in harmony with the ideas of the right hemisphere. But in time it came to be swept away by the large-scale, rootless, mechanical force of capitalism, a left hemisphere product of the Enlightenment.[21]

The Ego Explosion

As mentioned in the previous chapter, in his book *The Fall,* Steve Taylor explores a shift that took place some 6,000 or so years ago which caused an Ego Explosion. An increasingly definitive sense of ego-self formed along with civilisation, as it was needed to plan ahead, analyse and manipulate. There are obvious correlations to the rise of ego-consciousness and the shift to alpha thinking from original participation and the increasing dominance of left hemisphere attention. Like left hemisphere awareness, the egotistic self is a re-presentation, a mental abstraction that we develop as a tool for interacting with the world. It is like a split personality in that it separates a sense of 'I' from our true nature and then projects this 'I' as the mental image of ourselves as a defined, discrete 'I' dislocated from the world around us. Whereas a sense of 'I' is important for our personal development, analysis and planning, it becomes potentially abusive when consolidated into a projection that subsumes how we naturally are. Just as the left hemisphere is a vital assistant to the right hemisphere, the ego is a vital inclusion of our true Self. The tragedy comes about not because of the existence of the ego but when 'assistant' considers it to be 'master' and so the fragmented self becomes the dominant way of attending and our true Self suppressed.

Like the left hemisphere's incessant grasp gripping tighter in moments of uncertainty, ego-consciousness dislocates 'present' from 'past' and 'future' in order to critique 'what is' and make plans for 'what isn't yet'. The content of reality becomes over-analysed and extracted from context. While learning from experience and making appropriate alterations is vital for human evolution, the dislocated egotistic mind can become self-fuelling in its search for a problem to solve. Past learning becomes burdened with guilt and future planning burdened with worry. If ego-consciousness becomes dominant, it soon becomes a continual stream of mental chatter which breeds and recycles anxiety, narrowing down attention in a way that induces profound psychic suffering. Just as excessive left hemisphere awareness reduces our empathy and heightens our competitiveness through a narrowed down attitude, ego-consciousness sees the 'I' as separate and in fearful competition with others and life, breeding a self-fulfilling and self-deluding anxiety of over-analysis based on a detached, abstract view of reality. Moreover, a culture that breeds this anxiety and alienation further exacerbates this dis-eased state collectively and individually. Our attitude of mind becomes one of 'having', 'wanting', 'owning', 'consuming'.

According to Taylor, as ego-consciousness became more entrenched during the formation of early civilisations it drew more and more conscious energy away from our awareness of inclusion within Nature, hence coming hand-in-hand with our sense of estrangement. The apparent benefit of increased analytical capability came at a cost of reduced vitality and a growing sense of discontentment and incompleteness. As we dislocated from the World Soul and our true nature we felt we had to struggle for existence, through analysis, competition and warfare. This sense of struggle exacerbated ego-consciousness as our sense of vulnerability and level of anxiety increased. Yet more conscious energy was diverted to ego-consciousness in a vicious cycle of anxiety. We began to rationalise and narrow-down more and intuit and empathise less. The alpha thinking of ego-consciousness with its over-active left hemisphere grabbed more and more of the conscious energy to meet the perceived needs of the anxiety it created, and then further exacerbated. It contributed to what we explored in the previous chapter as the dominator model of social organisation forming around fear, control and domination. Taylor notes:

> At the very core of our being we are one with the universe, infinite and eternal, beyond space and time and death. Although we have become alienated from this true nature, we still have an intuition of it, and our deepest drive is to regain the wholeness we have lost. However, we go about this in completely the wrong way, and translate the characteristics of our true spiritual nature into the realm of the ego.[22]

To summarise our findings in Part One, we have explored how over time our Western worldview has tended towards a narrowed-down, fragmented and mechanistic perspective that undermines our relationship with our selves, each other and Nature. The Scientific Revolution was an important period whereby such a logic came to dominate, with its origins deeply woven into Western civilisation. This dominant view of how the world works has come to tyrannise and delude us, creating an illusion of separation which sends us down the path of rampant competitiveness and consumerism. In Part Two we explore ways of attending that help thin the veil of this delusion so that a deeper reality may be glimpsed.

Part Two:

The Thinning of the Veil

7. Nature's Ways of Relating

Thou, Nature, art my goddess; to thy law my services are bound.
William Shakespeare[1]

As we have seen, in 1857 Charles Darwin's ground-breaking work set the scene for defining the unit of ecological evolution as the organism separate from, and in competitive struggle with, its environment. This is what Gregory Bateson viewed as the basic flaw which corrupts the thinking that flows from it. In reality, nothing is separate from its environment, everything engages through energetic and material relation with its surroundings.[2] All the time new findings bring fresh perspectives to how we view the intricate workings of Nature. For instance, great discoveries have been made at the molecular level. Far from the genome being an innately selfish and rigid set of building blocks, we now realise it is a fluid dynamic system in continual interplay with its environment. Rather than dog-eat-dog competition, the driving force behind evolution appears to be cooperation and reciprocal interrelations. In the words of biologists Lynn Margulis and Dorion Sagan, 'Life did not take over the globe by combat, but by networking'.[3] Let's take a closer look at Nature's enchanting ways of relating, starting with the living cells within us.

Content in dynamic dialogue with context

In Nature every living organism consists of one or more living cells. The interior workings of these cells are contained within a watery milieu of protoplasm by a fluid envelope called the plasma membrane or cell membrane. So vital is this living cell boundary to the ability of each cell to stay alive and relate in a sustainable and variable way to its neighbourhood, that some biologists have likened it to a cell's 'brain'. It is the differential permeability of this envelope to water and water-soluble and insoluble substances that enables it to play this vital role. It is a semi-permeable enclosure containing pores or channels through which substances can flow into and out from the cell interior. Some substances have to be pumped through it by means of an energy-demanding process called 'active transport'. The use of energy in this way is associated with the development of an electrical potential difference between the cell interior and its surroundings. Cells can only remain alive so long as this potential difference is sustained. Without it, the chemistry within and surrounding the cell would simply equalise and the integrity of the cell as a self-sustaining identity would collapse.

For living cells to stay alive, their envelopes must be sufficiently permeable to allow substances that provide energy to flow into them, but not so permeable as to immediately lose whatever they have gained (like a bucket full of holes). They need, therefore to sustain an appropriate and variable balance between permeability and impermeability, which is sensitive to their environmental circumstances. For many years biologists thought the role of the cell membrane was passive. More recently there has been increasing recognition of the role of surface 'receptors' (signal-receiving molecules) that reconfigure in response to stimuli and bring about changes in permeability that can lead in turn to changes in cell function. As cell biologist Bruce Lipton observes, 'membrane receptors respond to both physical and energetic environmental information'.[4]

The presence of a boundary between the inner world and outer world of a living system does not isolate it from its environment as a discrete or 'independent' entity, but is vital to sustaining its identity as a dynamic inclusion of its environment. Life breathes through the continual inspiration-expiration of energetic flows through permeable boundaries. There can be no hard-line boundary around any living form, yet there is most definitely a boundary. Sometimes in our eagerness to dispel the illusion of separation, we seek to do away with boundaries all together, viewing everything as an amorphous 'oneness' where dualism is replaced with monism. In doing that, we replace paradox with paradox – we are all the same yet obviously different. In reality, there is no either/or. It is not the presence of the boundary itself that is causing the dualistic corruption of reality; it is our rationalistic desire for a clean-cut, hard-and-fast boundary separating content from context. Boundaries abound yet hard-line boundaries are abstract illusions. There is differentiation and distinctness yet there is no absolute discreteness. It is what the naturalist poet William Wordsworth pointed out two centuries ago when he said, 'In Nature, everything is distinct, yet nothing defined into absolute, independent singleness.'[5]

Sensing and responding in Nature

Life is continually expressing itself through open dialogue with life. Organisms pulsate in a relation of continual dynamic tension with the world around them; they are always adjusting, rebalancing and shifting to environmental perturbations.[6] Receptors in the organism convert sensory signals into electrical impulses. These electrical impulses provide a detectable electric and magnetic field around the organism as do sensory organs, like the heart. There is a sea of EM wave energy being given off by all aspects of the environment, living and non-living. Our bodies are in continual EM dialogue with much remaining out of reach of our normal conscious awareness. The philosopher Christian de Quincey notes that:

> We are constantly sharing messages with the world around us, picking them up in our bodymind, processing or metabolizing them, and expressing some residue back out. We call this process 'life' ... As the self opens up to respond to more environment – whether physical, mental, or spiritual – the experience of self expands and more of what was not-self is incorporated.[7]

The ability of each 'bodymind' to open up and filter this continual dialogue is fundamental to how the organism survives and thrives.

The health of the organism greatly relates to the electromagnetic interactivity and resonance of the organism with its environment. EM fields influence physiological processes: enzyme activity, cell growth, tissue repair, and so on.[8] As we have seen, each cell membrane surrounding the cell is a semi-permeable boundary with thousands of pores that open and close depending upon what is being sensed. With EM fluctuations, the membrane can either become more permeable and, in turn, more sensitive yet more vulnerable to its environment, or it can become less permeable and, in turn, less sensitive and more protected from its environment. The membrane is continually detecting, decoding and experiencing subtle changes in EM wave form, amplitude and frequency.[9] Nature is continually attuning its ability to sense and respond. In opening up to this continuous stream of sensory flux flowing all around and through us, we embody this interactivity of Nature; we attune within this ocean of ebbing and flowing energy. In becoming consciously aware of swimming within this ocean of energy we may begin to experience Nature beyond the fragmenting separation of abstract rationality. The magic of Nature flowing through the relations as well as in the things themselves is overlooked by the lens of objectified science. There is reciprocity between body and world where the perceiver and environment are not independent but interactive; cultural and environmental factors interact and reciprocate with personal factors.[10]

Diversity is the spice of life

Reciprocal relationships ensure that each living being gains energy and resources through the ocean of relationships within their ecosystem. The more reciprocal relationships there are, the more tolerant or 'playful' the ecosystem is to social, economic and environmental change. Diversity improves the chances of creating reciprocal, co-creative relationships. Monocultures, on the other hand, occur when one type of species or one type of organisational or cultural behaviour is encouraged at the expense of others. Such monocultures reduce diversity and the chance for reciprocal relationships to form, making their members more vulnerable to collapse – as when a hitherto unknown disease spreads like wildfire through a uniformly susceptible population.

In Nature, we find the formations of monocultures at the outset of ecological succession, following a disturbance or disruption to the ecosystem. Certain organisms capitalise on this disturbance – prolific species referred to as 'weeds' and 'rodents'. Interestingly, these organisms exhibit similar characteristics to human capitalists – short-termism, focus on rapid growth, exploitation of immediately available resources, formation of monocultures, inability to associate and sustain themselves in complex relationships with others, and so on. Just as interesting, many mammalian males tend to exhibit more of these capitalist characteristics than their female counterparts who tend to focus more on nurturing reciprocal relations. These capitalist characteristics are natural expressions of Nature; yet when these characteristics become dominating to the extent of undermining Nature's unfolding richness, then disharmony ensues, with hyper-capitalist, patriarchal, dominator cultures tending towards unsustainability. Excessive competition and short-termism destroys diversity and innovation – a lesson it seems that many politicians, company executives and economists have yet to learn. It's about time we started to wake up to the wisdom running throughout life on Earth – our ability to work with rather than against each other and harmonise the tensions of competition and cooperation. By way of exemplifying the inspiration Nature can provide us, let's take a look at what lies in the soil beneath our feet, a place we often overlook for inspiration.

Inspired by soil

Soil is a vast repertoire of hidden life – millions of microorganisms can be found in just a teaspoon of it. The living community in one teaspoon of healthy soil includes 100 million bacterial cells, hundreds of metres of fungal hyphae, 10,000 protozoans, and a similar number of algal propagules, as well as larger microarthropods, nematodes, and worms – each playing important roles in the living ecosystem of the soil. Soil lives in symbiosis with plant life, each helping the other in their cycles of life. The soil provides the vital reincarnation process of death and decomposition into new life. A handful of soil has many millions of bacteria in it with complex networks operating through semi-permeable membrane boundaries. Since the Archeon – some 3,500 million years ago – bacteria have been thriving on Earth through networks and partnerships spanning the entire globe. Bacteria cells continually re-invent themselves as they attune with their environment through what is referred to as 'autopoiesis' or self-making, which is a form of co-creating with their environment. Bacteria often live in vibrant communities with different cells carrying out different functions while all working together as a super-organism – a group of organisms communicating and collaborating together, adapting to their surroundings in a coherent way that benefits all the community.[11]

Bacterial communication is known as 'quorum sensing' which they use to detect helpful and harmful situations, activating dormant genes, switching language where needed to obviate disruptive behaviour. Communicating throughout the community allows them to form mixed species communities and so increase their diversity and the variety of tasks undertaken, therefore becoming more resilient during times of volatile environmental conditions. If bacterial behaviour detrimental to the community is detected, through quorum sensing those 'anti-social' bacteria can be 'tuned-out' of the community 'discussion' and so left with the option of addressing their incompatible behaviour or being excluded from the benefits of being part of the community. It is as if there is a bacterial social intelligence.[12] According to holistic scientist Stephan Harding, bacteria are deeply sentient creatures that work together creatively with exquisite sensitivity to their environment.[13] Interestingly, many self-serving relationships within bacteria communities have evolved into mutualistic relationships as if recognising the enhanced benefits of partnership. As Harding notes, 'The great bacterial web has run the planet to this day, and is, in a way, rather like the unconscious processes that operate key aspects of our own metabolism ... our very own cells are associations of once free-living bacteria that now engage in sophisticated intra-cellular communication.'[14]

As well as bacteria in healthy soil, we find fungi – or networks of mycelia as called by biologists. Mycelia are the builders of soil and the grand recyclers of life. Their fine web of cells run through the soil unlocking nutrients from one source and providing food for another. Fungi specialist Paul Stamets views mycelia as the neurological networks of Nature. In his book *Mycelium Running,* he explains that mycelia form vast sentient networks of information-sharing membranes, 'These membranes are aware, react to change, and collectively have the long-term health of the host environment in mind'.[15] Breaking down decaying matter into nutrients for life as they go, they share the nutrients across wide ranges of diverse ecosystems and in so doing help ensure the overall health of these diverse ecosystems. Mycelia display four modes of activity: exploration, assimilation, conservation and redistribution. As these sentient networks explore for nutrients in the soil they expand outwards in a radial fashion. While assimilating nutrients they also conserve other areas of the wider ecosystem by redistributing nutrients throughout their network. Mycelia networks can, for instance, connect one tree of a certain species, say an oak, with another tree of a different species, say a beech, and share nutrients between them where one tree may be rich in one mineral where the other is deficit.

It is vital these networkers simultaneously let go of their communication and nutrient network structures while holding on to current nutrient supplies. Too much holding on can result in gridlock – an overly retentive system that gets caught up in the density of its own self-integration and so cannot move on. Too much letting go can lead to dissolution and a lack of capacity for sharing, communicating and learning. Vital to mycelia – or for that matter all of life – is this attunement of holding on and letting go within an ever-transforming context. Giving is essential for receiving. Death provides the opportunity for life. Reconfiguration enables fresh exploration. Letting go allows for thresholds to be crossed and perceived boundaries to be transcended.

Forester Suzanne Simard has been exploring the soils beneath our feet for many years and has found extensive mutuality amongst bacteria, fungi and plants. Far from life being driven by an innate competitive struggle it partners and relates to form richer environments for life to further evolve. 'Facilitation ecology' is a growing area of interest for ecologists who study how facilitation happens between species at an ecosystem level. Traditionally we assumed that species would become more competitive as environmental conditions became tougher, but from recent studies it seems many species becoming more cooperative in stressful times. Rather than organisms struggling for survival they thrive through dynamic relationship. Western science is beginning to recognise that evolution is essentially co-creative, fluid and variably connective; something animist cultures have intuitively known for millennia. Our own bodies are a good example of the extensiveness of interplay and partnering that goes on throughout the biotic world as only one out of every ten cells within our bodies is actually human. Without the help of the 'friendly' bacteria within our bodies we would utterly fail at life. It is also worth noting that in times of strife, like the hurricane-induced flooding in New York for instance, we humans often transcend perceived boundaries of separation and seek to help each other where possible, and so there is hope even with our culturally habituated ways of thinking so deeply ingrained in separation, scarcity and competition.

Non-local sensing and responding

There is a 'non-local' way in which Nature relates, which is undefinable within the limitations of materialist science, yet has been proven time and again to occur. Detectable sensing and responding seems to occur instantaneously regardless of locality, for example, telepathy and synchronicity. This topic is as rich as it is deep, and worthy of a book in itself, yet a couple of examples are offered here to provide some insight into this seemingly mysterious yet detectable 'non-local' way of attending.

Mind focus

At the Mind Science Foundation in Texas, William Brand and Marilyn Schlitz have undertaken rigorously controlled experiments on telepathy.[16] A 'receiver' person's brain wave patterns are recorded while a 'sender' person meditates on telepathically sending a message. The experiments proved that, regardless of the spatial distance and EM conductivity between them (often the receiver was in a Faraday Cage to prevent any detectable EM waves being transmitted to the receiver) changes occurred comparable to mental processes in the receiver's brain shortly after the sender started to 'transmit' – it seems to take a few moments for the 'sender' to concentrate strongly enough or 'tune in' for the transmission to successfully happen which then seems to occur instantaneously. Similar experiments have been undertaken to examine distance healing where patients feel 'energetic' effects shortly after healers 'transmit' healing at times unbeknown to the patients. There seems to be a channelling of energy beyond detectable EM frequency happening in a non-local way. It is not distance but intention and quality of attention that determines success.

Animal communication

Another example of non-local sensing and responding is animal communication such as horse whispering. Anna Breytenbach is one such inter-species communicator who uses intuitive information to engage in two way conversations with animals. Mental images appear to her either as visions, thoughts, sudden knowings or phrases which relay what the animal is trying to communicate. She then, through her intention, sends a message back to the animal. Breytenbach's communication skills have been verified through various experiments where time and again she has gleaned very specific historic information previously unbeknown to her about the animals. Interestingly, this communication can happen remotely. All that is needed is a photograph of the animal and the communicator can tune into the 'energetic signature' of the animal and so communicate in a non-local way, for instance, from another country. Breytenbach, like many other animal communicators, has been helping animals in distress with impressive results for many years, while also helping the animals' owners become aware of the sentience of their animal kin. Breytenbach likens her intuitive skill to how indigenous people develop a sense of kinship with the natural world. As Carl Jung explored, it seems intuition has a creative potential which operates beyond the realms of classical physics: intuition, he said, 'is not mere perception, or vision, but an active, creative process'.[17] Breytenbach is very clear that we all have this innate capability to intuitively sense and respond with the natural world, and so attune with the wisdom of Nature. For her, our sense of separation from Nature detrimentally impacts our innate intuitive awareness. Reawakening this latent potential, she says, is as much a journey of the heart as it is the mind, and allows us to find our true empathy for our fellow kinship in Nature.[18]

Plant empathy

Another quite different yet related example of non-local sensing and responding is the amazing story of Cleve Backster, the CIA interrogation specialist who turned his lie-detecting attention to plants. Using polygraph instruments, which measure electrical resistance, he recognised that some plants seem to readily react to the emotions of humans. Backster recorded dramatic changes in electric patterns in plants which seemed to be triggered by his intention to harm the plant. For instance, when he made a decision, a clear intention to burn a leaf, the plant would react in a way that was picked up by the lie-detector.[19] He also found that it seems plants respond in sympathy to the death or pain of other beings. For instance, his lie-detector picked up dramatic reactions from the plant when live shrimps were dropped into boiling water. As he explored further, he found that certain plants seemed to respond differently to calm or loving people than to agitated or aggressive people. He published results in *The International Journal of Parapsychology* in 1968 which were subsequently verified by other laboratories.[20] From this biologist Lyall Watson noted:

> Plants lack a true nervous system or a brain. But their ability to store and carry memories, and their capacity for meaningful communication, suggest that the mechanics of information transmission and retrieval may be far more fundamental than many scientists now believe.[21]

New animism

The British scientist Rupert Sheldrake has been exploring such non-local phenomena for many years. He has developed a concept of morphic resonance, where morphic fields animate organisms at all levels of complexity. This 'hypothesis of formative causation' (first proposed in 1981) suggests that all self-organising systems (be they living organisms, societies of organisms, or crystals, for instance) exhibit morphic fields and through a process of morphic resonance these fields are influenced. Morphic resonance does not fall off with space, like influencing forces in classical physics, as they do not transfer energy but information, and so have a non-local sensing and responding characteristic. Organisms (and other self-organising systems like crystals) can pick-up or inherit habits from others through morphic resonance instantaneously regardless of distance. And so collective memory of past habits and present behaviour of organisms can affect current and future behaviour and so contribute to evolution. Sheldrake's theory appreciates the importance of DNA and other proteins in organisms, but it also recognises the role of influences from outside, from other organisms which are transmitting information with appropriate resonance. From this point of view, living beings inherit not only genes but also morphic fields and interrelate through these morphic fields with past, present and future behavioural implications. Clearly, there are similarities here to how animist peoples have long perceived the world, hence why Sheldrake refers to his theory as 'new animism'.

Individuals and the collective have a reverberative influence upon each other as the dialogue of sensing and responding happens both individually and collectively. It seems from scientific research that as animals learn new things a new 'behaviour field' is reinforced by morphic resonance which affects not only the animals learning but also similarly attuned animals who then engage in a similar task. The 'collective learning' becomes instilled within communities of similarly attuned organisms in ways beyond that of normal epigenetic modification. To help explain this morphic resonance concept, Sheldrake uses the analogy of the TV set. The TV can be affected by component faults (analogous to genetic defects) but the TV set components cannot explain the pictures broadcasted for the evening news report. These pictures are not produced by the TV set's components. Likewise, genetic defects or mutations can affect an organism's form and behaviour but its overall form and behaviour is no more purely genetic than the TV programme is governed by the components inside the TV. For Sheldrake, it is morphic resonance that provides the broadcast transmission. As organisms we are tuned in to certain transmission frequencies, that of a human or that of a fly, for instance. Yet, we can also attune ourselves to resonate in a more conscious and open way with wider Nature through the quality of our attention and intention – rather like tuning into different news broadcasts – and so enhance our ability to sense and respond in non-local ways, whether that be inter species communication, telepathy or distance healing.

Ancient traditions have long understood each psyche as exhibiting a subtle energy system influencing consciousness in non-local ways. Our limited senses and ego-consciousness conceal what is a deeper cosmic connectivity. Each distinct and collective psyche has its own memory and resonance. As we open up, or rather tune-in (like Sheldrake's TV set analogy) we allow this deeper nature of reality into our conscious awareness. In the words of the psychiatrist Stanislaf Grof:

> I see consciousness and the human psyche as expressions and reflections of a cosmic intelligence that permeates the entire universe and all of existence. We are not just highly evolved animals with biological computers embedded inside our skulls; we are also fields of consciousness without limits, transcending time, space, matter and linear causality.[22]

This non-local consciousness can provide optimism for what lies ahead of humanity, as synchronistic attunement between like-minded people across geographies may allow for a threshold of awareness to be crossed with new ways of attending spreading contagiously in non-local ways. It is what the old alchemist proverb, quoted by Jung, points to, 'No matter how isolated you are and how lonely you feel, if you do your work truly and conscientiously, unknown friends will come and seek you'.[23]

8. Quantum Reality

Let there be light.
Genesis[1]

In the mid-nineteenth century, James Clerk Maxwell explored how electricity, magnetism and light are all manifestations of the same phenomenon: what became known as 'the electromagnetic field'. He examined how electric and magnetic waves travel through space perpendicular to each other within a field of electromagnetic light. He revolutionised physics with the finding that disturbances in one region of the field could propagate via electromagnetic waves. His work is often referred to as the second great unification in physics after Newton's first, and his discoveries ushered in a new era of physics known as quantum physics.

Meanwhile, Einstein's theories of special and general relativity helped transform the prevalent worldview of matter as discrete blocks in space by examining the relationship of matter and energy and of space and time. Einstein proposed an all-pervading field – a space-time continuum – within which the entire universe exists. His addition of time as a fourth dimension of reality was revolutionary for its day and his examination of matter as energy was equally groundbreaking. Particle physicist and Nobel laureate Steven Weinberg helped further transform our perception of space, time, energy and matter when he asserted that it is fields, not particles, which make up the universe. The concept of matter as the be-all-and-end-all of life appeared no longer valid. Far from matter being the fundamental building block of our universe, we find that matter is not actually matter at all.

In the early twentieth century, Einstein along with Max Planck, Walter Nernst and others explored the notion of a zero-point field quantum vacuum (QV) which exhibits a background hiss of electromagnetic (EM) energy that pervades the entire space-time dimension. In fact, this QV is now viewed by some quantum scientists as being an infinite source of energy which can be accessed at any point within our universe – if we had the capability, we could tune into all the energy we need, and more, right here right now. This all-pervasive infinite light energy is unperceivable to us as beyond the range of frequency that our senses can detect, so we cannot notice it, yet it is supposedly everywhere. It is perhaps a good job we cannot notice it as it could easily overwhelm us if we were able to tune into it. A useful analogy to imagine this quantum reality is this: we are living deep underwater with the sea all around being like the all-pervading ocean of energy in our midst. Much like a fish does not consciously sense the water it lives in, we do not consciously sense the QV ocean all around us, yet it is there.

More recently, astrophysicist Bernard Haisch and others explored the relationship of matter and inertia within this QV energy field. In Haisch's words, the 'underlying sea of quantum light' is what gives matter its solidity.[2] According to Haisch, all matter is a form of EM vibrational energy originating from the QV field. Matter is vibrating energy that appears as solid matter to us yet is actually projections of energy from the QV field. It seems it is light (which is what EM is) that fills the space-time dimension; this seemingly solid world of objects which we interrelate with are now regarded as light-filled projections. Our creation as we perceive it is formed from charged, polarised energy projecting particle-like from the uncharged background sea of quantum energy.[3] Haisch explains:

> Picture a snowflake with its fine crystalline pattern; picture an igloo with its solidity; picture an ice sculpture with its form. Snowflakes, igloos, and ice sculptures are all made from water, which, in its normal state, has no form at all.[4]

This quantum vision of reality transforms everything we knew of life and enables us to explain the interrelatedness of life we may sometimes intuit. It is as if the observable universe floats upon the surface of this quantum field, like foam on the surface of water. We see the bubbles yet do not observe the water beneath. To perceive the superficial 'bubbles of matter' as all there is, is to neglect the enormity of the ocean without diving beneath its surface.

Wave-particle duality

During the nineteenth century light became understood by scientists as waves; light waves caused behaviour such as refraction, diffusion and polarisation. In 1900, Max Planck developed the notion that light could be mathematically treated as particle-like as well as wave-like. This helped with mathematical calculations. A few years later Einstein proposed that light actually was both wave-like and particle-like not just for calculation purposes but in how it behaves in reality; the quantisation of light into packets. These light packets became known as photons which displayed both wave and particle properties. In 1924, Louis de Broglie proposed that matter, like light, has both wave and particle-like properties. This wave-particle duality became an important principle of quantum theory and Dirac, Pauli, Bohr, Heisenberg, Schrödinger and many other notable scientists developed upon this wave-particle principle in their quantum theory work. In 1927, Eddington suggested the word 'wavicle' to describe this phenomenon.

Universal Vibration

String theory (or super string theory and its extension, M-Theory) is a relatively recent theory much in vogue among quantum theorists. Here, particles are not understood as 'matter' in the conventional sense rather they are packets of vibrating strings which create localised vibrational fields that appear to us as particles. Different dimensions within string theory are defined by different frequencies of vibration; moving up a dimension is like moving up a harmonic in music or tuning into a different radio or TV station broadcasting at a different frequency.

Non-locality is a quantum theory which explores activities between particles of energy that appear instantaneous across space. Something is said to be 'local' in physics when it is connected through space-time via an identifiable force or signal. Hence 'non-local' activities transcend the conventional limitations of physics by operating beyond our classical view of space, time, energy and matter. It is as if these 'wavicles' or 'strings' interrelate somehow beyond space and time. It is thought that the unifying QV pervades all of space and so connects these 'non-local' activities. This helps explain phenomena such as telepathy, distance healing and extra-sensory perception, the measurable effects of which have long been viewed as unscientific as the causes are undetectable by classical physics even though scientific study groups have proven their effect in repeatable and verifiable ways.

One of the founding fathers of quantum physics, Paul Dirac, described the QV as a dance between antimatter, matter and light. Recent cosmic discoveries allude to 'dark energy' pervading the universe much like the QV concept. Many leading physicists now believe that without this unseen all-pervading 'dark energy' life would not exist, much like the ripples and bubbles would not exist without the turbulent water beneath the surface. Some scientists have been exploring the notion that our universe is actually holographic and that the interference patterns of the ripples upon the QV surface we call reality have stored information. Within a hologram the image of the whole can be reproduced from a fragment of it – the whole is contained within the parts as each part contains information on the whole. Some physicists view the universe as a big hologram with each ripple on the QV containing the image of the universe. Physicist David Bohm called this 'holomovement' in which light flows into matter and back into light again and where any part of the universe is a partial realisation of the relationships within the whole universe. In this regard, the universe can be viewed as a rich sea of consciousness, a holographic web of information. No longer is space viewed as nothingness, it is a buzzing field through which all activities originate and seemingly unconnected particles interrelate in non-local ways. String theorist Michio Kaku proclaims that the mind of God is 'music resonating through hyperspace'.[5] This begs the question posed by scientist Manjir Samata-Laughton: 'Is every note of that music imbued with an inherent sentience?'[6] Imagine for one moment, each 'wavicle' of vibration within every aspect of reality is sentient.

Far from space being empty, according to these views, it is what brings matter into being and enables it to interact and take part in evolution. It leads us to realise the universe is a receptive medium that births and sustains form. It points to that receptive medium containing and permeating all forms. Thus we can no longer view matter as primary and space as secondary, as it is space (or ocean) which allows reality to come into existence. The cosmologist Brian Swimme describes it as 'the all nourishing abyss'.[7] This makes for a universe that is more than 'interconnected' as rather than discrete parts connecting through point relations everything is immersed within, through and of an all-pervasive oceanic presence. Everything is vibrating expressions of this abyss; each vibration imbued with a unique frequency. As Haisch alluded to, each snowflake is unique yet all are of water. We are all continuously interrelating with the waves, eddies and vortices in our midst. Perhaps rather than 'interconnected' a better way of describing this is 'interrelated' as the ocean does not really connect but rather flows throughout everything.

The concept of an all-pervading field (or receptive ocean) may be gaining ground in Western science through the discoveries of quantum theory, yet it is not new to humanity. Ancient cultures have long recognised the existence of an all-pervading presence. For instance, in the Indian Upanishads the Source of life is known as Akasha, with Prana the all-pervading life-force that emanates from within Akasha. Akasha underlies all of creation and contains memory of the self-creating universe through the 'Akashic record', much like an ocean retains memory of what happens upon its surface through the ripples and waves formed. Perhaps shamans, seers and mystics enter the QV by tuning into levels of consciousness beyond our normal realm. The scientist and philosopher Ervin Laszlo noted that:

> The dance of our mind with the quantum vacuum links us with other minds around us ... it opens our mind to society, to nature, and to the universe. This openness has been known to mystics and sensitives, prophets and metaphysicians through the ages.[8]

The scientific recognition of an all-pervasive presence flowing through our physical reality provides an opening for materialist science to re-engage with its spiritual past. Eastern philosophies and ancient esoteric wisdom blend with Western science to provide a richer view of reality.

Multiple realities

A recent development in quantum theory has been the Variable Speed of Light (VSL) Theory put forward by a group of physicists led by Joao

Magueijo that suggests light is infinite, with our universe's specific dimension of reality existing at the frequency we call the speed of light, and with other dimensions or universes existing at different frequencies than the speed of light. VSL purports that the speed of light in our dimension is only a limitation of our perception within this dimension of reality.[9] Other dimensions of reality exist right here, right now but we cannot sense them as they operate at different frequencies. Back to our analogy of radio or TV stations broadcasting at different frequencies. We know that there are many TV and radio stations broadcasting simultaneously, but as we tune in we pick up a specific radio signal or TV channel. VSL states that light slows down from higher frequencies in order to form our dimension of matter and anti-matter along with space and time as we perceive it in this universe. The limit of our perception is bound within this dimension, known as our 'Perception Horizon'. Beyond our Perception Horizon lie universes beyond our realm of matter accessible through higher frequency consciousness. Consciousness is not limited by matter and so could transcend the Perception Horizon and go beyond the speed of light – non-locality and Sheldrake's morphic resonance may be conceived in this way.

Spiralling new beginnings

The Black Hole Principle (BHP) put forward by scientist Manjir Samata-Laughton, in her book *Punk Science,* builds on quantum theory and VSL by examining recent discoveries of black holes. More and more black holes are being discovered throughout our universe. Previously they were assumed to be energy sinks which pulled in light and destroyed matter, hence why they appear dark. The opposite is now being considered. There is evidence of black holes emitting jet streams of high frequency electrons much like scientists think would have occurred at the early stages of our universe being formed shortly after the Big Bang whereupon anti-matter and matter were forming from light. It may be that these high frequency electron streams are formed from light beyond our Perception Horizon (at a frequency beyond the speed of light so undetectable by us) which then creates antimatter and matter in the form of electrons as it enters our Perception Horizon. Far from black holes being energy draining destroyers, they may be the creative sources of our universe.[10] The moment light arrives from beyond our universe it enters black holes slowing down its frequency and transforming into antimatter and matter. It is thought that light forms a spiralling vortex as it makes its way through the black hole from a higher dimension into ours. The spiral is an intrinsic pattern of creation found at all levels from the DNA double helix within each cell of our bodies and the spiralling blood flow within our veins and arteries to spirally cosmic nebulae interstellar formations. On closer inspection we understand that vortices and spirals form to reduce resistance by curving inwards and so reducing the confrontational resistance of straight line motion. The spiral pattern has long been revered by ancient mysticism and indigenous wisdom as well as being examined by pioneering Western scientists and inventors such as Nikola Tesla, Wilhelm Reich and Viktor Schauberger in the quest for the fundamental driving force, or dynamic energetic presence, found throughout Nature and the cosmos (see Figure 8.1).[11]

Figure 8.1: The primordial spiral.

Anti matter and matter

Nobelists Tsung Dao Lee and Cheng Nig Yong explored the concept of antimatter and matter existing in parallel to each other, one as a mirror image of the other. Matter exists at a lower frequency (the speed of light, referred to as 'c' in physics) than antimatter (the speed of light multiplied by itself 'c^2') It is thought that light beyond our perception horizon forms antimatter at c^2 frequency and then matter at the lower frequency c, which is what we perceive as our dimension of reality. This mirror universe of antimatter could explain the existence of 'dark matter' and 'dark energy' which scientists believe exist in our universe. Paradoxically, if we could sense the dark energy it would be far brighter and more energised than our dimension; it seems we inhabit the lower frequency dark side. The beauty of anti-matter and matter is that they exist in a state of continual dynamic interplay, antimatter forming matter forming antimatter again; continual co-creativity as the unifying dynamism of cosmic and biological reality.

Our ever-deepening view of reality is still barely peering beyond the meniscus of its surface, yet as preconceived boundaries of space, time, matter and energy begin to dissolve, we bring into view aspects of reality beneath and beyond the surface. Western philosophical rationalism and scientific reductionism with all its efforts to define and categorise reality has succeeded in piercing its own illusionary certainty to glimpse at phenomena which have long since been explored by mystics, alchemists and shamans for millennia. Modernity meets the ancient.

9. Beyond Dualism

Contrary to the dominant Western view extending from Plato and Aristotle to Averroes and Aquinas and culminating in Descartes, the knower is not divorced from the known, the inner from the outer, the self from the world. We are enabled to know the so-called outside world only because something of that outside world (anima mundi) is also inside ourselves.

Roberts Avens[1]

Through the ages many Western philosophers have grappled with the relationship between: psyche and physical; transcendent and immanent; mind and matter. As Western philosophy tended towards rationalism and materialism, a sense of separation formed between what is viewed as conscious mind above and beyond inert matter. Spirit became divorced from Nature. Nature became nature with a small 'n' as it was no longer imbued with a divine quality, it was de-sacralised into a collection of objects, the motion and interaction of which could be defined through objectified materialist science. While this has been the defining trend of Western philosophy and science, greatly impacting our cultural and socio-economic models, there have been many exceptional Western thinkers challenging the separation of mind and matter or psyche and physical. The Western philosophy of phenomenology, as we shall explore in the next chapter, has been influential in helping to challenge the illusion of separation by emphasising the 'inbetweenness' of relations and the inter-subjectivity found through our empirical experience of phenomena. In this chapter, we make a brief exploration into three important schools of thought tackling the material and spiritual interrelation in Nature: these are panpsychism, pantheism and panentheism. But first, we turn our attention to consciousness itself and how at the end of the nineteenth through to the mid-twentieth century, notable Western philosophers explored the spiritual dimension of reality around the same time that Western scientists embarked on quantum theories. While there have been many profound philosophical contributions, the conceptual thinking of the following philosophers is specifically relevant here: Henri Bergson (1859–1941); William James (1842–1910); Alfred North Whitehead (1861–1947); Charles Hartshorne (1897–2000); Pierre Teilhard de Chardin (1881–1955); David Bohm (1917–1992).

Henri Bergson was an influential French philosopher who explored creative impulse, subjective experience, intuition, time, evolution, mind, creativity and freedom amongst other themes. He found that matter exhibits degrees of consciousness: as the complexity of self-organisation in matter increases so does its ability to perceive and memorise. He developed the notion of 'elan vital' as a creative impetus within evolution. For Bergson, consciousness is a universal phenomenon with individual beings displaying their own uniqueness yet embodied within this universal consciousness. And so Nature is imbued with Mind. He saw consciousness as a dynamic psychical expression which flows through all matter, animating it to varying degrees of complexity. Throughout his writings he used image and metaphor to help engage the reader beyond the purely rationalising intellectual realm which he viewed as incomplete abstraction, providing – at best – snap shots of reality rather than the real thing which is intuited through our contemplative embodiment of this universal consciousness. For Bergson:

> ... intuition starts from movement, posits it, or rather perceives it as reality itself, and sees in immobility only an abstract moment, a snapshot taken by our mind, of a mobility. Intelligence ordinarily concerns itself with things, meaning by that with the static, and makes of change an accident which is supposedly superadded. For intuition the essential is change: as for the thing, as intelligence understands it, it is a cutting which has been made out of the becoming and set up by our mind as a substitute for the whole.[2]

Bergson became friends with the influential American philosopher, William James. James became supportive of Bergson's theories and, like Bergson, James viewed materialism as morally defective as it sought to eradicate intimate relations embedded within reality. James noted, 'Reality, life, experience, concreteness, immediacy, use what word you will, exceeds our logic, overflows and surrounds it.'[3] James envisaged a transformation towards a worldview where experience and reason meet and the material and spiritual realms entwine. He said:

> Our normal waking consciousness, rational consciousness as we call it, is but one special type of consciousness, whilst all about it, parted from it by the filmiest of screens, there lie potential forms of consciousness entirely different. ... No account of the universe in its totality can be final which leaves these other forms of consciousness quite disregarded.[4]

For James, the mind-world relation is a stream of consciousness; God is the universal mind and we are all conscious participants within that Mind. James is widely regarded as one of the most influential philosophers in the United States and his thinking helped shape subsequent approaches to psychology and sociology.[5]

The British philosopher Alfred North Whitehead, as Professor of Philosophy at Harvard, reviewed much of the philosophical thinking of that day. He was greatly influenced by Bergson's philosophy and the latest quantum theories emerging at that time. He viewed the world as a sea of interrelated processes. All matter has a level of mind, or 'prehension' as he called it, from the subatomic level to humans. He proposed that both the mechanics of matter and the dynamics of consciousness relate to an inherent creativity within the universe that gives rise to reality as we perceive it. Hence matter and consciousness is a process; temporal rather than spatial. Reality is made up of experiential events which Whitehead called 'occasions of experience'. Mind or consciousness is a process, much like James spoke of the 'stream of consciousness'. There is no separation of consciousness and matter. As the present day philosopher Christian de Quincey puts it:

> ... mind is the intrinsic, purposeful self-motion of matter ... It is not some external force or substance acting on a body ... Mind is neither outside nor inside matter, but is constituent of the very essence of matter – interior to its being.[6]

Interestingly, this view of matter as imbued with psyche harks back to Neo-Platonic, Aristotelian, Platonic and Pre-socratic thought largely lost with the advent of the Cartesian paradigm. For Whitehead, life is a dynamic open-ended process of creativity, a process of 'becoming'. Our wisdom grows through this process of becoming. The primary task of philosophy for Whitehead was to reconcile science and religion – also philosophy and theology – by rethinking the universe as an open-ended spontaneous, creative, living network of interactions, unfolding through a conscious process. Consciousness, and so meaning and sense of purpose, is viewed as flowing through all of matter and throughout Nature. The divine animating principle of Nature is re-found and with it Nature re-sacralised. His philosophy founded the movements of 'process philosophy' and 'process theology' where reality is viewed as a dynamic unfolding process; everything in life is alive, relational and continually co-creating new possibilities.

Building on much of Whitehead's process philosophy was the American philosopher Charles Hartshorne who developed a comprehensive process philosophy of religion. The present day process philosopher David Ray Griffin explains:

> The goal of process philosophy of religion ... is to provide a new worldview that can be seen by the scientific community, the philosophical community and the various religious communities to be *more adequate* than previous worldviews ... In Hartshorne's words, 'the fallacies in the older proofs were largely due to the attempt to justify an erroneous conception of God.' In agreement with most atheistic philosophers, process philosophers hold that that conception was, if not internally incoherent, at least morally problematic and in strong tension with several features of the world as known through modern science.[7]

Hartshorne viewed all matter as sentient, with the capacity for feelings like sympathy, enjoyment and love. Every particle and every activity is in intimate relation with the world; this co-creative free-will he explored in relation to the Divine.[8]

The unfolding truth

Definable static truth can be satisfactorily grasped through abstract rationality yet may lead to a false sense of reality – an illusion – unless adequately counter-balanced with a more experiential, intuited and embodied perception of reality.[9] As the process theologian Catherine Keller asks: 'What if truth itself is a way not an endpoint? What if the way and its truth deliver no totalizing absolute – nor deliver us to the indifferent dissolute? What if we have here to find a third way?'[10] As we transcend our dualistic mind-matter way of viewing the world we reveal a truer version of reality beyond the dualism of either/ or. The 'third way' Keller points to is of truth as an ungraspable co-creative relational unfolding process, a progressive journey rather than a static thing. The campaigner and writer Satish Kumar observes, 'Truth is not a "correct" belief system. It is not a point of arrival: it is a continuous process, a continuous search and a continuous way of being.'[11] Truth: not as a noun nor a verb but a participle; a dynamic, ever-unfolding way of being, a becoming. Truth, in its splendid feral dynamism, is beyond the controlling, artificiality of rationalism's desire to put-upon-the-rack, tie-down, abstract and dissect. Truth is, to use Keller's words, an unfolding of 'open-ended interactivity'[12]; it 'isn't a neon revelation but a revealing illumination'.[13]

French philosopher, palaeontologist and Jesuit priest Pierre Teilhard de Chardin developed a visionary metaphysical system. The theologian professor and biographer of Teilhard de Chardin, Ursula King, considers him to be one of the great Christian mystics of the twentieth century due to his quest for a new vision that conveyed the interrelatedness of spirit and matter. King notes that he was not only a man of ideas but of passion seeking to unify heart and mind. His deepest desire was to seek the essence of things within the rhythm of the cosmos.[14] For Teilhard de Chardin, spirit and matter are both within and of the other (rather like the yin and yang of Taoism), two aspects of the same reality. He viewed the consciousness of mind or spirit as an evolutionary process in all things; an increasing intensity as evolution unfolds through complexity of relations. He noted, 'From the biosphere to the species, all is but an immense ramification of psyches searching for one another through forms.'[15] Influenced by Bergson, Lamarck and Darwin, Teilhard de Chardin believed there was an evolutionary energy that carries matter towards increasingly complex and intricate organisation. This development of organisation within organisms came with the development of the psyche, an increased sentience which he referred to as conscious 'interiorisation'. And so he saw evolution as a transformation of psyche. For Teilhard de Chardin, each vibration of energy has a 'psychical kindling or concentration'.[16] The universe unfolds through a 'pulling' of creation towards an Omega Point. The universal process of evolution is a becoming of mind through ever-greater depth of intensity, culminating in Christ-consciousness whereby the Divine becomes conscious; this is the Omega Point for humanity. For Teilhard de Chardin, the formation of Christ's body is found throughout Nature – the Divine as both transcendent and immanent within which we are immersed. Unfortunately, the Catholic Church severely reprimanded him for his work. In 1947 the Church forbade him to write or teach on philosophical subjects as viewed it as containing 'errors' offensive to the Catholic doctrine. Subsequently, however, both Pope John Paul II and Pope Benedict XVI have made reference to his profound work.[17]

The American quantum physicist David Bohm explored the philosophical implications of quantum physics with regard to the relation of mind or spirit and matter. He understood there to be a 'universal process of becoming' underlying all matter.[18] His theory of 'Implicate and Explicate Order' explores how the immanent realm of energetic form manifests within a co-creating ocean of energy enfolded within the unmanifest transcendent spirit realm. The process of manifestation is through what he called 'holomovement' – the continual enfolding and unfolding participatory process of becoming. He concurred with Whitehead's process philosophy that Nature has an aliveness permeating through all aspects of it. He saw mind as present at the sub-atomic level. He referred to the quantum wave-function of sub-atomic particles as a 'dance' exhibiting consciousness and he recognised the participatory nature of this dance; particles (or 'wavicles') dance together to a greater or lesser degree depending on their participatory interaction with each other. This participation, for Bohm, occurs both within the mind and matter realm which are aspects of the same phenomenon.[19] During Bohm's last decade of life he brought this theory directly into practice through workshops on in-depth dialogue, including the recognition that dialogue can serve humans well by bringing forth shared meaning.

Participatory consciousness

A cosmic Mind enacting through human consciousness in a participatory way is not new to the West, with Presocratics such as Heraclitus and Parmenides hinting at such. More recently, Goethe viewed the intra-subjectivity of events as participatory in an intrinsic and transpersonal way, and following on from this was Rudolf Steiner's anthroposophy. And a couple of decades ago, astrophysicist John Archibald Wheeler explored the notion of a participatory universe, building on Bohm's and others' concepts. For Wheeler, we are the eyes through which the universe looks at itself. Inspired by this work and the concepts of Teilhard de Chardin, Bergson and others, the Polish philosopher Henryk Skolimowski developed a theory of Participatory Mind published in 1994 which has contributed to an increasing interest in ecological philosophy. Skolimowski's aspiration is that the objectification of Western materialist science, which he views as having led to the ecological, social and economic crises in our midst, can be transformed by this participatory understanding of consciousness whereupon humans have reverence for all relations in becoming conscious of the interrelated participatory nature of life.

Holistic scientist Stephan Harding in his book *Animate Earth* explores how our sense of relation with Nature is embedded within our consciousness. It is often lurking just below the surface of our rational mind's grasp and with a slight shift in awareness we can tap into it. This reigniting of our vital relation with Nature re-enchants and replenishes us, allowing us to re-perceive the world as it really is beyond the illusion of separation. For ecological psychology (which we explore in the next chapter) this shift of awareness has been referred to as a shift from ego-consciousness to ecological consciousness whereupon we perceive the aliveness of the interrelating way of Nature, which in turn allows for a sense of reverence for all of life. This ecological consciousness perceives the animating life force flowing throughout Nature and is what indigenous people have been aware of for millennia. Interestingly, from a Western perspective, the Pre-socratic philosophers of Hellenistic Greece viewed Nature in this way too. And so this ecological consciousness heralds a return to participatory consciousness, much like Barfield explored in his theory of the evolution of consciousness from original participation through alpha and beta thinking into final participation.

Norwegian philosopher Arne Naess explored the ethical implications of this ecological consciousness in what became known as the deep ecology movement. Deep ecology is an ecological philosophy which over the last few decades has gained increasing influence in the West. The word 'deep' is used to convey the point that it views ecology in a deeper way than the prevailing Neo-Darwinian worldview. For deep ecologists, Nature is far more than a collection of minerals, food and manufacturing inputs to be utilised by humanity, rather every aspect of Nature plays its part within a rich, dynamic unfolding. From this ecological worldview ethical considerations on how humanity relates within Nature can form. As the writer and cosmologist Thomas Berry famously said, 'The universe is a communion of subjects not a collection of objects.' In becoming consciously aware of our embodied participation in the world, we can either choose to work with the grain of Nature or work against it, we can either help heal our world or continue to plunder and pollute it. This is what Berry refers to as 'the Great Work' where we transform ourselves from plunderers to benefactors.[20] It is what Satish Kumar points to when he says, 'without reverence there can be no ecology, and without spirituality there can be no sustainability.'[21]

Panpsychism

Panpsychism is a philosophical theory that views all matter as conscious, originating from the Greek words *pan* meaning 'everywhere' and *psyche* meaning 'soul' or 'mind'. All particles have an inner nature, a living subjective quality not just chemical and biological but also a form of conscious awareness. Human consciousness is viewed as a subset within a universal consciousness which pervades all material things. Hence, seemingly inert matter (for instance, a stone) exhibits a form of consciousness, a mind-like quality. Panpsychism has philosophical roots in the Pre-socratics with Thales and Empedocles among others exhibiting aspects of panpsychism in their thinking, and it clearly relates to animism (as well as pantheism and panentheism which we explore in a moment) which has roots reaching way beyond Hellenistic philosophy into Neolithic Europe and further afield, as we have seen. According to the panpsychist philosopher David Skrbina:

> Panpsychism appears able to provide the foundation for a new worldview in a way that deeply addresses the root issues. It is easy to abuse dead, inanimate matter, or unconscious forms of life. The human who alone has mind, or in whom mind is a contradiction or unfathomable mystery, has no sense of being at home in the cosmos. As a consequence he is likely to feel alienated, frightened, angry, or foolish. It need not be so. Philosophers have envisioned alternative views that have equal claim to validity. We as a civilization need only summon our collective wisdom and courage, learn the lessons of history, and transcend the crude, destructive, and ultimately dehumanizing materialist worldview.[22]

Pantheism

Pantheism literally means 'everything is God'. As a theology it purports that the sacred is present in everything, or that God's essence is in everything and God is immanent within everything; 'all is God' and 'God is all'. In orthodox Christianity, pantheism was and is considered a heresy, partly because pantheism does not acknowledge God's transcendence of Nature. Traditional theism views God's divine omnipotence as determining all events, with God perceived as a transcendent male deity, above and beyond His Creation. With pantheism, every aspect of the universe is considered Divine, and all material aspects exhibiting God as Oneness. Some theologians point to logical and spiritual inconsistencies in pantheism. It would take considerable exposition to enumerate these, yet to point in the direction of those critiques consider these concerns: Pantheism is of this world; God is logically understood in terms of necessity and finitude; notions such as infinity, transcendence, creativity and freedom at best feel uncomfortable within pantheism; humans and other species seem trapped in determinism. These kinds of theological problems gave rise to a major break in understanding the nature of the sacred: Pan-en-theism.

Panentheism

Panentheism is an understanding that 'everything is in God, and God is in everything'. Pantheism, where God is the world, or the universe, differs from this because panentheism recognises and accounts for the presence of an unknown and unknowable mysterious, infinite, intangible and transcendent realm that interacts with all that can be experienced, named and known. (Mahayana Buddhism has this too, in the tradition of Nagarjuna, with the mutuality of 'Thingness' and 'No-Thingness', that is, Sunyata. This also relates to the concept of the all-pervasive 'Tao' within Chinese philosophy.) The divine presence of God in panentheism is both immanent in creation and also transcendent beyond it as the primordial soul from which the World Soul originates. Each and every moment is imbued with consciousness as a loving, holy presence. And so God could be called Nature, or Abyss, or No-Thingness, yet God is beyond names or metaphors. Panentheism, as a theological philosophy, grew out of German idealism, but it has a long developmental history that reaches back to ancient Indian and Egyptian sources, to the ancient Chinese Lao Tzu, to Greek philosophy and Platonic thought, to Jewish-Christian Scriptures and Sufi Persian mysticism. Panentheism holds that theological and philosophical polarities – such as yin-yang, feminine-masculine, immanent-transcendent, freedom-necessity – need to be included within the divine being; and that monism needs to be replaced by a di-polar expression of non-dualism. Notable panentheist thinkers of the past century include Martin Buber, Albert Schweitzer, Alan Watts, Alfred North Whitehead, Pierre Teilhard de Chardin and Charles Hartshorne. Contemporary panentheist process theologians include John Cobb, Jr., Matthew Fox, Carol Christ, Mary Elizabeth Mullino Moore, David Ray Griffin and Catherine Keller.

Participatory evolution

What we have seen from exploring Nature's ways of relating, quantum theories and Western schools of thought, is that far from our bodies being disembodied, as they are in Descartes' mind-divorced-from-matter philosophy, our bodies are resonating within a flux of interrelations. We are engaged within a continual dialogue of sensing and responding through the semi-permeability of ourselves with each other: intuiting, sensing and rationalising through our interactions. As de Quincey says, our bodies are 'embedded and embodied' in this matrix of relationships.[23] For de Quincey:

> Meaning, not mere mechanism, becomes the connection between beings; synchronicity, not causality, patterns these meanings and connections – and the cosmos as a whole resonates to the creative meaning of its own never-ending story, a narrative of ensouled matter and embodied experience, embracing the sublime paradox of "subjective objects", of multiplicity-in-unity.[24]

The universe can be understood as a co-creative process of participating. The manifesting process of life is an organic participation. We recognise the importance of pattern and relation as unfolding 'content' flowing within an interrelated 'context'. Nothing is isolated. There is no separation, only differentiation. To separate content from context (whether at the sub-atomic level or at the organism level) is to attempt to sever life from its organising influence, its Mind or Soul. We are essentially flowing as a process of becoming through our 'being-in-the-world', as the philosopher Martin Heidegger would say. Perceiver and perceived are co-participating, and each presence in our local (and non-local) neighbourhood is pulsating within a sentient ocean. In the words of the Indian philosopher Sri Aurobindo:

> If it be true, that Spirit is involved in Matter and apparent Nature is secret God, then the manifestation of the divine in himself and the realisation of God within and without are the highest and most legitimate aim possible to man on earth.[25]

10. An Awakened Way of Relating

Man knows himself only to the extent that he knows the world; he becomes aware of himself only within the world, and aware of the world only within himself.

Goethe[1]

Phenomenology

As the nineteenth century drew to a close, the German philosopher Edmund Husserl – often thought of as the founding father of phenomenology – felt that the Cartesian philosophy and empirical scientific methodology of the day failed adequately to account for the nature of experience. By emphasising the role of empathy, embodied experience and intuitive feeling he sought to transcend the objectification of Western science. Through an 'inward' experiential understanding Husserl felt the world could be more truthfully understood, and so he formulated phenomenology as a philosophy. The Greek word *phainomenon* means 'that which shows itself', not the mere appearance of something, and its intellectual analysis, but the revealing *experience*.[2] In phenomenology, 'experience' is not just the sensory qualities of our experience (seeing, hearing, and so on) but also the significance and meaning they arouse such as empathy, imagination, bodily awareness and embodied action. These forms of experience are what Husserl referred to as 'intentionality' which occurs *through* a given experience and makes up its meaning. His philosophy was greatly influenced by Goethe's way of seeing, Stumpf's work on sensory experience and Hegel's conceptual thinking on the phenomenology of consciousness. Husserl's assistant, the German phenomenologist Martin Heidegger, further developed upon Husserl's work.

Heidegger felt that Western philosophy had misunderstood what it meant 'to be', to really experience something rather than rationally abstracting an understanding of it. For him, a return to practical engagement with reality through lived experience allowed for an 'unconcealing' of reality. Heidegger viewed the objective, abstractive perception of the rationalist-empiricist as an 'unworlding' of the world, a denaturing which gives a sense of something lacking, a sense of wanting in us, caused by our fractured perception.[3] Heidegger's student Hans-Georg Gadamer and the French phenomenologist Maurice Merleau-Ponty further enriched phenomenology with their own profound insights, as have many others since. Interestingly, Gnostic knowledge of ancient times was rooted in a way of knowing found in the embodiment of the phenomenon through the relation of the knower and the known rather than conceptual knowledge 'about' an objectified theory. For the Gnostics, perception through the empirical, the imagination, intuition and direct perception through the heart were highly valued as well as rational logic. Likewise ancient animist cultures engage shamanically with phenomena. And so the heritage of phenomenology reaches back into our mystic and animist history.

The animating presence of awareness

Maurice Merleau-Ponty called phenomenological experience a direct and primitive contact with the world whereupon we experience a 'being-in-the-world', a synergy or communion with reality as our existence continually unfolds. He understood perception as a 'mutual embrace', a conversation between body and world reigniting our vital embodiment within Nature. For Merleau-Ponty there is no experience, perception or self-knowledge without a world to interact with. He viewed the intimacy of our body-world relation like the inhaling and exhaling of air, restricted only by the reflective abstraction of our minds.[4]

As we have already explored, our bodies are semi-permeable organs of perception in continual dialogue with the environment. We are continuous with the world we perceive. We are always being sensed by Nature just as we sense and interact with our lived-in world around us, which is flowing through us as a co-creative empathic resonance (sometimes attuning with consonance, sometimes dissonance, often a blend in-between). Our bodies and minds are not in any way separate from Nature, they are reverberating with and through our sensory perception. Merleau-Ponty referred to this animating sentient presence as 'Flesh'. 'Flesh' can be seen as a sensuous flow through both the perceiver and the perceived. As the perceiver and perceived sensuously relate they form a participatory mutual embrace.[5] It is what the cultural ecologist David Abram refers to as 'the reciprocity of the sensuous', as if 'the world is perceiving itself through us'.[6]

Presencing

For both Heidegger and Merleau-Ponty to 'presence' is to immerse within the 'now', the primordial dimension beyond the spatial or temporal, where the space and time of a moment is transcended into a sacred presence of full-bodied awareness.[7] The present expands into a presence, an immersion within a vibrant awareness beyond abstract isolation. Heidegger used the word *'worlding'* to express an energetic aliveness as a dynamic presence of the world – presencing as a process.[8] Presencing is achieved by shifting the focus of attention within experience away from 'what' is experienced into the experiencing of it, the empathic unfolding of the experience.[9] As we focus our attention on the phenomenon in a heartfelt, embodied, presencing way – what Goethe refers to as 'active seeing' – our perception develops into an active beholding of the unfolding experience within its lived-in ever-changing context. For Goethe, to observe Nature one requires a certain purity of mind free from preoccupation, judgements or concerns about the past or future. Goethe's active seeing goes beyond the senses, it is an intuitive seeing whereupon the interrelated, metamorphic, intensive depth of the phenomenon is perceived.[10] As phenomenologist Cheryl Sanders-Sardello explains:

> To be here requires attention, listening, and gazing deeply without assaulting each thing seen with a conclusion. The silence here is not just in the 'what has been', it is most deliciously waiting, too, in the 'what will be'.[11]

Within this state of presence – what Eckhart Tolle refers to as *The Power of Now* – our personal psyche opens into a deeper intelligence;

our mind attunes within the reverberating Mind of Nature or World Soul. Presencing in this way is a rich, profound experience, quite beyond words. The deeper we immerse ourselves in this aliveness, the deeper our awareness becomes – we attune and get into the flow of Nature, what some people refer to as getting into 'the zone'.

It is here that we comprehend what Confucius pondered some five centuries before Christ when he said, 'He who is in harmony with Nature hits the mark without effort and apprehends the truth without thinking'.[12] This state of presence is with us always, no matter of space and time, as it is beyond space and time; it is our true underlying reality and allows us to perceive content as participating within context. With the assistance of this phenomenological way of perceiving, each moment can be viewed as an opportunity for presencing, an aperture into deeper receptivity. Interestingly, when we seek to control, analyse and manipulate this unfolding participation the state of presence is lost; we close down the co-creative flow with our narrow-mindedness. As Tony Parsons, author of *The Open Secret*, poetically puts it:

> In our rush to find a better situation in time, we trample over the flower of beingness that presents itself in every moment … Presence is our constant nature but most of the time we are interrupting it by living in a state of expectation, motivation or interpretation.[13]

For Parsons, presencing is a spontaneity born from stillness. Learning to embrace our own stillness within and all around us is the gift of presencing, what Parsons calls the open secret where 'existence either blossoms in that presence or reflects back my sense of separation'.[14]

Sharing beyond separation

Rather than perceiving something as an object or subject we relate as a presencing experience with empathic 'betweenness'. This allows for a sharing; a relating with 'other' and so a healing of any sense of separation from 'other'. We become aware of a flowing receptivity between ourselves and our neighbourhood. We can perceive a receptive *and* responsive, spatial *and* energetic, right brain *and* left-brain, heart *and* head relationship with reality. The sharp, definitive edges of polarised dualities are washed away as we empathise with life. We become expressions within, rather than separate from, Nature. Yet, importantly, we still maintain distance, differentiation and relativity through this empathic relation. Heidegger referred to this reciprocity with the world as 'authenticity'; where one becomes authentically engaged within the world by fully engaging 'through' our senses. We start to perceive the world as it really is – spatially and dynamically continuous. This helps us shift from a purely self-centred, competitive, power-hungry, manipulative engagement with our world to an empathic embodiment of our world with which we are in continual communion.

Ecopsychology

Ecological psychology (ecopsychology for short) studies the relationship between Nature and humanity. Ecopsychology studies the benefits of dissolving the sense of separation from Nature inherent within the Western mindset. In the words of ecopsychologist Andy Fisher:

> Ecopsychologists argue that genuine sanity is grounded in the reality of the natural world; that the ecological crisis signifies a pathological break from this reality, and that the route out of our crisis must therefore involve, among other things, a psychological reconciliation with the living earth.[15]

Research shows that people gain emotional nourishment and enhanced well-being, as well as increased levels of concentration, intuition and creativity, through a healthier engagement with Nature: for instance, studies at the University of Wisconsin where gall bladder patients looking out on to Nature recovered significantly faster than those with no view of Nature; and the Chicago metropolitan district regeneration programme where neighbourhoods with easy access to Nature recorded significant reduction in dysfunctional behaviour and depression. Yet, ecopsychology is quite different from environmental psychology. Environmental psychology seeks to understand and value the benefits Nature has on the human psyche – enhanced health and wellbeing – while often still perceiving Nature as a kind of 'resource' for human betterment, needing to be measured and conserved because of this anthropocentric value, and so leaving the human-Nature separation largely unchallenged. For ecopsychology, according to Fisher, human-Nature integration is its main calling.[16]

Excessive abstract rationality and egotism hardens the sense of 'I' sealing it within its 'interior' whereupon Nature is perceived as 'exterior'. With this sense of separation comes a diminishing reciprocity of inner-outer.[17] We become detached from our sensuous participatory embodiment of our surroundings by becoming too much in our ego-minds. Our psyche fragments into a 'domesticated' conscious awareness and an unconscious 'wildness'. Domestication and wildness are aspects of the same continuum inherent within us. If either domestication or wildness predominates then the individual and collective culture can get out-of-kilter.[18] In the West, domestication, monoculture and control suppress wildness and the challenge we face is to rectify this balance through our inner-outer and conscious-unconscious attunement. This is what ecopsychology aims to achieve by exploring greater attunement of our human-Nature awareness. We can allow a more expansive state of consciousness and a more porous sense of self to occur through presencing. As we presence we become consciously aware of a heartfelt commingling of felt presences. This is Merleau-Ponty's reciprocal interplay of perceiver and perceived where content and context are understood as co-creative of each-in-the-other's aliveness. This embodiment is an ongoing participatory emergence as the moment unfolds. Attaining such a state of awareness is to begin to embrace what shamanic people experience when attuning with consciousness beyond the realm of the self into the realms of other humans, animals, plants and beyond. This state of 'shamanic consciousness' comes with an increased sense of reverence for all of life, along with a reduced sense of separation.

11. Awakening the Self

Emancipate yourselves from mental slavery; none but ourselves can free our minds.

Bob Marley[1]

Individuation

Carl Jung was a visionary psychoanalyst who studied in detail the workings of the ego-self in relation to the 'Self' – our true essence. Jung's 'Self' transcends the ego and is a human manifestation of the World Soul. The journey of self-realisation is a developmental process of unfolding within oneself through a relaxation of our ego-defences as we open up to the world; a germinating process of breaking through our 'I' encapsulation to permeate with the inner soil of our true essence. This echoes Aristotle's and Plato's (as well as many other great philosophers') goal of discovering one's truth. It is a process of becoming our destiny which Jung called 'individuation'.[2] For Jung the goal of life is the realisation of one's own true nature through individuation.[3] This comes with the integration of all aspects of our psyche by allowing our unconscious to become conscious, which can be a lifelong journey. While becoming a fully-conscious Self may be nigh on impossible for many of us, except for the likes of Buddha and Jesus Christ, by merely embarking on the journey of conscious awareness one gains a sense of profound meaning in one's life and with it a deep attunement with Nature's wisdom. This is the quest for divine illumination seen by Pythagoras as the ultimate goal of philosophy. For Jung, without the inner understanding and wisdom that individuation brings we are without meaning, adrift in a volatile, windswept world clinging to material possessions for illusory meaning and fickle happiness. Jung saw consumerist society as indicative of a lack of authentic meaning; aimlessness at the collective and individual level.[4]

Jung recognised that repressed aspects of our psyche (our shadow) are projected on to others through our inner-outer way of attending. As we consciously integrate aspects of our dark shadowy depths by acknowledging and integrating these aspects into our conscious awareness, we embrace a fuller truer Self. In other words, by embarking on a journey to 'know thy Self' we individuate. As Jungian analyst, and author of the book *Jung*, Anthony Stevens notes:

> To individuate is to realise one's personal existence as a unique expression of humanity and, within the frail vessel of one's little psychic world, to distil the essence of creation. In this microcosmic experiment the great cosmos becomes conscious of itself.[5]

The conscious mind is reliant upon the unconscious psyche for its fuller expression; so too is our human ego-consciousness reliant on the deeper ecological and cosmic consciousness of Nature for its fuller expression. And so we find that this self-Self attunement comes with a rarefying of the ego as it becomes more permeable to the World Soul of Nature: a self-other-Nature attunement.

Jung considered that the individuation journey has a dynamic tension within it which creates an oscillating, spiralling process of transformation. As we are driven outwards and onwards we are pulled inwards and seemingly backwards. Hence, the transformational journey is far from linear or predictable; it is more like a spiral of progressive and regressive twists and turns with each twist providing deeper knowing along the way. Ecopsychologists David Key and Margaret Kerr visualise the transformational journey as a triple spiral form, a triskele – an ancient symbol found in indigenous cultures around the world (see Figure 11.1 on page 114).[6]

Key and Kerr refer to the three aspects of the triskele as: the divided spiral, the embodied spiral and the unified spiral, with a liminal zone in the heart of the triskele. Within the divided spiral, the process of self-realisation spirals towards a release whereupon the dominant ego begins to perceive the world as no longer separate from and in competition with it. The move out of this first spiral can often be traumatic as deeply embedded ways of being start to be left behind. As the ego-self softens and opens, becoming less isolated and more

Figure 11.1: The triskele.

permeable, the process of transformation moves on to the embodied spiral where we start to let go of the incessant desire to rationalise and intellectualise our experiences of the world. We find ourselves becoming more open to sensory and experiential ways of attending. This comes with a more creative, playful and improvisational way of relating along with a deeper interrelation with the natural world as we reawaken our ancient shamanic consciousness. Again this spiralling transformation comes with ever-increasing permeability of our ego-boundaries. Then as we transform through the unified spiral we gain greater awareness of flowing within the all-surrounding presence of Nature. The ego-self is a differentiated, yet also a transpersonal, expression within the deep matrix of Nature, not superior to or separate from other beings but swimming within the same oceanic immersion that flows through everything.

Each journey round the spiralling triskele allows previously unconscious phenomena to emerge into conscious awareness and so become accepted as a meaningful part of a new experience of self. Each transition from one spiral to the next requires a crossing of a threshold – a breakdown and breakthrough phase of death and rebirth – and so, with that, a period of unease, confusion and fear. There is no end point as such on the self-transformation journey only continual learning and self-realisation to bring further deepening of awareness, learning and understanding. We become more than we are through this learning process. Each situation in life can be perceived as an opportunity to learn; life as a continual learning experience, every cloud having a silver lining, every twist and turn bringing a deeper unfolding. It is only our preconceived judgements and conditioned fears that make us view situations and experiences as 'good' or 'bad'. It is what the psychologist Eugene Gendlin points to when he says, 'Every bad feeling is potential energy toward a more right way of being if you give it space to move toward its rightness.'[7] With this continual learning and opening up of our ego-boundaries, the ego's desire to usurp or control the Self wanes, finding comfort within its rightful place as useful assistant which serves a deeper, wiser awareness.

Meditation

An important part of the journey of individuation is quieting our busy minds. By quietening the chattering ego-mind we open up to our primal receptive awareness, the oceanic depths upon which our ego-consciousness floats. As Tai Chi specialist Peter Chin Kean Choy describes:

> With a quiet mind, feel yourself gently sinking down into your heart and listening to your heart valves pumping blood around the whole body. Listen to the pulsation of your heart, feel the pauses in between the heartbeats … .The more you listen to the spaces between your heartbeats, the more receptive you are to these 'limitless spaces'. You are literally touching this limitless space with all your emotion and with all your mind.[8]

This quietening of the mind meditation relaxes us into a state of receptive awareness. When we gain awareness of the cosmic sound of silence within us, we may then come by what Buddhists call 'pure attention'.[9] With this pure attention we gain awareness of our changing feelings, attitudes, moods and thoughts. We see them for what they are, short-lived projections.

Meditation is becoming more widely accepted in the West and

is increasingly being practised at values-based organisations where it provides benefits not only of increased awareness, happiness and morality but also improved performance.[10] With meditation our brain-waves change frequency, and our inter-hemispheric balance is regained. There are certain tried-and-tested practices such as Vipassana, Yoga Nidra, Transcendental Meditation, controlled breathing or chanting mantras, but these may seem out-of-the-ordinary in modern Western society and so may put some of us off. The good news is we can meditate while walking, jogging, sitting quietly for a moment, lying in bed, gardening or preparing dinner. Many of us may do it routinely, without needing to give it a label. The simple act of bringing our awareness into the present moment – such as becoming conscious of our breathing – can act as a window into a meditative state. It costs nothing to meditate yet it can bring life changing benefits.

Through meditation we observe thoughts and feelings that arise within us but let them pass by without our awareness getting too wrapped up in them; we surrender them rather than letting them engulf us. With dedicated practice, the mental chatter of the racing mind quietens and it becomes easier to notice superficial thoughts appearing. Simply allow the thoughts to come and go, and if we find ourselves getting involved, becoming consumed by a thought and going off with it, then, when we catch ourselves doing this, we can bring ourselves back gently to the point of witnessing thoughts. The trick is to not be too harsh on oneself. If we find ourselves engrossed in a thought or feeling then it is sometimes interesting to track back as to how the mind got to where it did. This can make us consciously aware of the way the mind so often gets caught up in wild goose chases building up worry and fear from often superfluous origins. Again gently bring the mind back. It may be helpful to think of the thoughts appearing as cars travelling along a road in front of us. As each car passes us we can either go for a ride, being taken off down the road of that thought where ever that may end up, or we can let the car pass by and remain a witness to the stream of traffic. The more we witness the mental chatter the more it quietens allowing stillness for our deeper consciousness to come through where, as Jung would say, our psychic quicksilver lies. This letting-go of, or release from, mental chatter is what Reverend Cynthia Bourgeault, of the Contemplative Society, refers to as *kenosis,* a 'self-emptying' or surrendering of our ego-consciousness, so as to be receptive to the Divine. Bourgeault points to the life-practice of Jesus Christ being rooted in *kenosis*. Put another way by writer Rashid Maxwell, 'Meditation is the tool for stepping away from the ego. It is returning to the ground of being from which existence springs. It is the wave remembering that it is not different from the ocean.'[11]

Initially, there may be some anxiety in going deeper as the ego-self starts to feel marginalised and so grasps anxiously to regain our attention. As we continue to let go, we come to a mental place of serenity which feels comfortable and quiet. With practice, one can go into this peaceful mental place and allow it to embrace the mind and body; with that a blissful sensation along with an exhilarating brightening of our deeper consciousness arises, like dawn breaking. This brightening steadily grows through practice and the mind can become illuminated by it, along with the heart opening within mind, and mind in heart. This can be the practice of a life time, and is what the Christian mystic Meister Eckhart referred to as opening the 'Eye of the Heart'.[12] It requires patience, dedication and courage, especially when we inhabit a culture full of anxiety, competition and lusting for superficial ego-gratification. It demands resistance to the values, expectations and falsehoods of that culture in order to follow an authentic path. This illuminating conscious state can bring discomfort as cultural norms and personal traits are challenged for what they really are. And yet it can also be immensely liberating as we shed our old skin and become free to dissociate ourselves from superficiality. Rather than moments of authenticity in a sea of inauthenticity, we can bring authenticity into all that we do. From here we can start to embrace the enchanting resonant beauty of Nature. We become conscious of the deeper soulful presence permeating within us, the imaginal realm.

The imaginal realm

The French philosopher-theologian, Henry Corbin, studied Sufi mysticism and coined the term *mundus imaginalis* (imaginal realm) to describe the existence of a realm that is not directly detectible through our bodily senses. Nonetheless, this realm is both imaginable and a real and potent presence in our everyday lives. The imagination required for being aware of this realm comes from more than mere speculative flights of fancy; it arises from *insight* – the ability to *infer* from or *see through* surface appearances to what lies deeper within and beyond those appearances.

Ancient cultures, such as the Egyptians, understood that divine illumination could be perceived through the phenomenal world with the aid of sacred imagination.[13] For the ancient Gnostic tradition, imagination is listening to the voice of the soul; so too for poets such as Coleridge and Keats where imagination is the reconciliation of transcendent qualities.[14] In the words of Coleridge:

> The primary imagination I hold to be the living power and prime agent of all human perception, a repetition in the finite mind of the eternal act of creation in the infinite I AM.[15]

For Corbin, imagination is the magical production of an image within our soul from which creative action originates.[16] The fertile soul-scape of the imaginal realm is where the spark of spontaneity spawns creativity infusing our conscious mind with cosmic consciousness. For Jung this is the unconscious becoming conscious, an animating power out of which everything of value is created.[17] This sacred imagination relates not only to our inner creative potential but also to our ability to relate to the world around us, providing for a deep sense of embodiment with life.

If we delve into the spiritual realms of many ancient cultures we find repeated references to an all-pervasive presence accessed through our soul which influences us through feelings, intuitions, dreams, and such like. Ancient Persian mysticism, like Jung's individuation, explores how the unconscious can be allowed to pervade our conscious awareness so allowing us to tap into a far greater potential, unlimited by ego-consciousness. Through meditation, prayer and other contemplative practices – such as expressive arts therapy, chanting, shamanic journeying, and so on – we can work at making the unconscious conscious by opening up our psychic being. We attend to that which is below the surface of our conscious awareness yet which may surface when we are in a relaxed state of receptive awareness; in Jungian psychology, this is called 'active-imagination'. As we become more practised at entering the dark fluid depths of our soul, the darkness starts to gain luminosity. This is reminiscent of the invisible wavelengths of electromagnetic radiation pervading our universe actually being a form of light vibrating at frequency beyond that which we can normally detect visually. It is also what ancient alchemists were intuiting, metaphorically, in seeking to discover how to transform base metal to gold – the dark depths of our true nature becomes illuminated as we transform through self-Self attunement.

Metaphorically, our living consciousness is like a limitless ocean and our immediate conscious awareness is us in a boat bobbing up and down on its surface waves. We can see and experience what is explicitly or tangibly going on around and above us and conclude that this is all there is to our lived-experience. Yet, implicitly, beneath the surface of the waves rocking us, there is actually much more involved, out of immediate sight and mind. We may, on a clear, calm day – with a relaxed mind – be able to see shafts of sunlight penetrating some way down into the watery depths below and perhaps catch the shadowy movement of something, yet the depths seem opaque, dark, mysterious, perhaps even scary. Our ego-consciousness is quick to fear the dark unknown, and unfortunately this fear then hardens the permeability of the ego-self and so shuts down the ability of the true Self to flow through into our conscious awareness. Yet it is very much there; the deep abyss within, throughout and all around us. We start to feel our creative potential flowing more freely as deep-seated psychic blockages or fears are allowed to surface and dissolve. Through this individuation, we can reconfigure our psyche, allowing a healing of fractures formed from supressed issues, past traumas and cultural conditioning. It is an immensely challenging process and yet also immensely rewarding. As the psychologist Annie Dillard warns us:

> In the deeps are the violence and terror of which psychology has warned us. But if you ride these monsters down, if you drop with them farther over the world's rim, you find what our sciences cannot locate or name, the substrate, the ocean or matrix or ether which buoys the rest, which gives goodness its power for good, and evil its power for evil, the unified field: our complex and inexplicable caring for each other, and for our life together here.[18]

As we start to attune our immediate and deep awareness, we also start to realise the full potential of who we really are and what our true life purpose is, a destiny that seeks to serve rather than sever; our way of attending becomes re-enchanted and revitalised.

To the Eyes of the man of Imagination,
Nature is Imagination itself.
As a man is, so he sees.

William Blake[19]

12. The Heart and Soul of It

And now here is my secret, a very simple secret, it is only with the heart that one can see rightly; what is essential is invisible to the eye.
Antoine de Saint-Exupéry[1]

The heart

Indigenous people throughout the world affirm that they have gained their ancient wisdom from their hearts which is where their soul-scape can be found. In contrast, the West prioritises rational logic over the receptive awareness of the heart. That said, many notable Western philosophers through the ages have recognised the importance of the heart's perception, such as Heraclitus, Bruno, Goethe and Steiner, and Western poets such as Eliot, Keats, Dante, Blake and Wordsworth, to name only a few.

What is well known in the West is that the mechanics of the heart pump oxygenated blood throughout our bodies to every single cell, beating a hundred thousand times a day without rest. Yet what is perhaps less well known is that the heart generates hormonal, chemical and electromagnetic messages throughout the body, directly influencing all organs including the brain. While the gastro-intestinal tract, or gut, and the human brain also give off and respond to electromagnetic messages, from studies it seems that the heart is the most powerful electromagnetic oscillator in the body. The electric field of the heart is forty to sixty times greater in amplitude than that of the brain and the magnetic field produced by the heart is more than five thousand times stronger than the brain's.[2] Sixty to sixty-five percent of all the cells in the heart are neural cells. These neural groupings within the heart directly connect with the body's nervous system, gut and brain. From research, it seems that the heart perceives things through its electromagnetic field before the brain does, then relaying messages to the brain which then relays back to the heart.[3] The pulsating heart provides an electromagnetic torus field round the body, influencing every cell and radiating many feet beyond the body (see Figure 12.1).[4]

Figure 12.1: A torus field and the human body.

All aspects of Nature give off these electromagnetic torus-shaped fields in varying degrees. For instance, plants and animals have detectable electromagnetic (EM) fields as does the Earth. All these EM fields interact in open dialogue with each other all the time. Some provide dissonance and others provide consonance for each other, or put another way, some are in-tune with each other where their combined effect provides stronger amplitude, others are out-of-tune with each other where their combination has a weakening overall effect. It is through our hearts that we can sense and respond most directly with these signals all around us, picking up subliminal or largely unconscious perceptions as well as opening up to our intuitive perception which then informs brain cognition.

Heart researcher Rollin McCraty has explored what happens when we allow ourselves to open up to the direct perception of the heart. As we attune with heart-focused perception, our eyes dilate, our peripheral vision increases and our focus becomes soft rather than acute, and our brain starts to entrain with our heart. Heart entrainment or heart coherence is when the brain functions start to synchronise with the heart. The EM waves of the brain embed themselves into the EM wave form of the heart. As coherence deepens, our emotional state becomes more relaxed, with a heightened sense of caring and affection, as well as a heightened perception of external stimuli. It is as if we become more alive and present within the moment through our hearts; we 'presence'. As our brain starts to align itself with the heart, the neural network of the entire body starts to synchronise as one wave form, with stronger amplitude – consonance. As researcher Stephen Harrod Buhner notes, this affects all aspects of our physiology: 'As coherence begins and deepens, the entire hormonal cascade of the body alters.'[5] The stress hormone cortisol drops down and there is a doubling in production of DHEA, a steroid which aids metabolic and memory functions, promotes feelings of well-being and enhances tissue repair and sexual hormone production. Notably, the hippocampus area of the brain enhances its functioning, stimulating stem cells to produce new neurons, along with neo-cortex activity in the brain changing as mental chatter reduces.[6] Overall, it seems heart entrainment shifts our conscious awareness from the forebrain region to the heart, which enhances well-being and physiological activity such as improved repair rates and immune system. It seems we start to heal ourselves as we open up to the perception of our hearts. The more often the heart entrains with the brain, the easier it becomes to regain entrainment time and again, and the healthier we become. The interrelations of the heart, brain and body mean that to assume the mind is associated only with the brain is incorrect. The mind is actually throughout our body and its pulsating torus field. This led biologist Candace Pert to coin the term 'bodymind' with the heart at its centre.[7]

Heart consciousness

Coherence of our thinking minds and intuitive hearts can be encouraged through practising contemplative awareness which allows our bodymind to find its centre; as Gerald May describes in his book *The Awakened Heart*, 'Contemplative practice is allowing the plumb line of one's being to find its place'.[8] Contemplative moments, no matter how fleeting they may be, are all-encompassing, open and expansive. It is a quality of presence beyond words where we directly perceive life beyond abstraction. It feels like a homecoming. May calls these moments of 'naked intuition' where 'everything is present at once, not merged together in a unified mush but resplendent in all its diversity ... And we are alive in it ... we are absolutely involved.'[9] We awaken to the enchantment of Nature – the early morning ray of sunlight passionately embracing the unfurling flower, for example, or the vibrant rainbow caught in a dew-laden spider's web. We become aware of what great poets like Dante and Rilke felt when they described the rhythms of Nature as flowing full of love. It is our awakened heart that opens us up to this quality of presence whereupon we consciously live within this love; and yet this love includes suffering and loss as well as joyful beauty and passion. Hence courage (originating from the Latin *cor* meaning 'heart') is required in opening to these ebbing and flowing tides of love. It is through our hearts, as Henry Corbin noted, that we feel, perceive and attend with sympathy and compassion, which allows for our authentic communing with others.[10]

Through the quality of our attention and our heartfelt intention, we affect our radiating EM (and quantum) heart field which not only affects the functioning of our brains and other body organs, but also affects others around us. This is how shamanic cultures throughout millennia have attuned with their neighbourhoods; it is how all our ancestors once lived. It is one thing to rationally understand that all of life is holistically interconnected in some way, it is quite another to deeply know through our hearts – this is wisdom. And so we may understand that heartfelt shamanic experience is a most profound philosophical experience.

The soulful reverie

You could not discover the limits of the soul, even if you travelled by every path in order to do so; so profound is its meaning.

Heraclitus[11]

The soul is not some 'thing' but rather it is a presence – a soul-scape – which we can access through our hearts. Poets, mystics, seers and shamans throughout the ages have attuned with this presence. It allows for what the imaginal psychologist Robert Romanyshyn in his book *Ways of the Heart* refers to as the 'presence of the poet', an elusive presence of otherness beyond facts and ideas where we allow the imaginal realm into our conscious way of attending. As Romanyshyn explains, 'In the imaginal realm of the heart, the flesh of body and that of world are a *con-spiracy,* a breathing together, an *intimacy* as close as the ties of love'.[12] We can be re-minded of the soulful presence beyond our ego-consciousness through everyday moments like bird song, rain drops falling, the breeze on our skin, even the feeling of our breath in and out of our nostrils which is always with us regardless of surroundings.

The French philosopher Gaston Bachelard used the word 'reverie' to explain such a soulful, poetic, contemplative way of perceiving. He said, 'Reverie is not a mind vacuum. It is the gift of an hour which knows the plenitude of the soul.'[13] Reverie is contemplative daydreaming which Bachelard likened to a flame – or light of the lamp – as it is not so much idle as passionately embracing the imaginal realm. For Romanyshyn, this reverie is a holding back, a pregnant pause within stillness, an oblique vision, a sideways or backward glance which indirectly alludes to a reality that is always elusive, beyond the grasp of ego-consciousness.[14] Soulful reverie lifts the veil of perception from our eyes for brief moments whereupon we expose ourselves to the mystery of the Divine. Romanyshyn talks of such a moment as:

> … an earthquake of the soul, a tear in the fabric of space and time, miracle ... to germinate in the recessed chambers of the human heart ... shimmering, resonating, vibrating frequencies which we, with our own poor consciousness, can tune into with only just enough awareness to be filled with longing.[15]

Empathic resonance

The word resonance has its root in the Latin *resonare* meaning 'to return to sound', to vibrate with the original pitch.[17] To resonate with the Divine through heartfelt presence is to flow within the currents of reality freed from mental abstraction. The phenomenologist Robert Sardello calls this 'empathic resonance' where the soul of the individual comes into resonance with the World Soul of Nature.[18] Perhaps the most profound way of finding this empathic resonance is through nothing more simple than silence; silence not only from the humdrum of today's busy world, but also from our own ego-consciousness with its associated mental chatter, prejudices and emotions, and also from the impressions of others and our collective cultural conditioning we have assimilated throughout our lives affecting the way we perceive.[19] Silence opens us up to what lies within our own depths, a soulful sacredness that flows throughout the cosmos. Sardello notes, in his profound book *Silence,* that this divine Silence is not a cessation of sound but what is prior to sound, already present.[20] This reminds us of Claude Debussy's famous quote: 'Music is the space between the notes'.[21] Silence is the receptive presence from which all energy – sound, light, movement, matter, and so on – is called forth. In Eastern mysticism, this all-pervading primordial Silence is the eternal Akasha or Tao. This Silence is ever present and always flowing through everything. In this regard, we could expand Debussy's insight by saying that 'the primordial silence of space is flowing between and through the notes'; the notes are themselves full of this divine Silence, resonating within it with their own frequency of note. A note viewed in isolation, abstracted from Silence, is a false fragmentation of reality; separating the note from the Silence is like separating light from dark or content from context or yin from yang, it leads to an artificial dualism, a corrupting illusion of separation. And so Silence can be seen as a presence of 'being' that is within the activity of 'becoming'. There is no need to hide from the world of noisy notes. If we learn to attune with the Silence flowing through everything, then the Divine can be perceived as flowing through each note as we go about our daily business.

13. Indigenous Wisdom

The Lakota could despise no creature, for all were of one blood, made by the same hand, and filled with the essence of the Great Mystery. In spirit, the Lakota were humble and meek. Blessed are the meek, for they shall inherit the earth - this was true for the Lakota, and from the earth they inherited secrets long since forgotten. Their religion was sane, natural, and human. The old Lakota was wise. He knew that a man's heart away from Nature becomes hard; he knew that lack of respect for growing, living things soon lead to a lack of respect for humans too. The old people came literally to love the soil and they sat or reclined on the ground with a feeling of being close to a mothering power.

Luther Standing Bear[1]

As we explored in Part One, indigenous peoples are shamanic cultures rooted in reciprocity and reverence for all relations throughout life from mountains and rivers to eagles and beavers. Within these ancient cultures, there is a deep heartfelt understanding that we are all part of the rich tapestry of life, if we cut one thread we weaken the entire tapestry. This is the ancient way of the heart that shows humility and respect for all relations. It is a wise way of attuning with Nature's rhythms that learns through our empathic interactions.

Indigenous wisdom views Nature as the Great Mother, the cosmic womb which nurtures and provides for the cyclic rhythm of life. In the great cycle of life all species and features of the landscape play their part, contributing to the Spirit. To ensure harmony within Nature, and so preserve the cycles of life, is innate within these ancient cultures. As the indigenous writer, Arkan Lushwala, explains 'It is true that we have great talents that other species do not have. But the purpose of our talents is not that the other forms of life serve us. On the contrary, the inherent purpose of our talents is to serve others.'[2] This is in stark contrast to modern Western culture which views Nature as a set of resources to be exploited for human gain. As well as a deep sense of reverence for all of life, indigenous cultures had (and still do have in many cases) a strong sense of self *within* community (human and non-human kinship), for instance a greater sense of sharing and openness than there is a sense of privacy or private ownership. This permeable sense of self within neighbourhood is notably different from the individualism now prevalent in the West. This open engagement through empathic relations in indigenous cultures ensures a sharing of resources and support, so reducing economic stratification. Although there is hierarchy within many traditional cultures, it tends to be one built on trust and earned respect rather than accumulated power and domination.

Sense of togetherness

Anthropologist Meredith Small notes, in her book *Our Babies, Ourselves,* that one obvious difference is the sense of togetherness found in babyhood, childhood and adulthood within indigenous cultures to a systemic sense of separation pervading all aspects of Western life, right down to the root – our sense of separation from Nature.[3] For instance, an indigenous mother sleeps with her baby at night and holds the baby next to her body during the day in a sling or such like. Western cultural norms have influenced parents to sleep separate from their babies to ensure a good night's sleep for the busy day ahead, and for the baby to be put in a pram, a play pen or in nursery where professional carers look after otherwise socially remote groups of infants to allow the parents to get on with meeting the demands of Western life. In the formative years of a Western child's life, talents are developed to give the child the best chance of 'success' in an independent, status-driven, competitive society desperately seeking happiness. Paradoxically, the sense of togetherness and lack of self-striving evident in indigenous cultures provides for happy people within vibrant, socially engaged, convivial cultures. Perhaps surprisingly, indigenous cultures historically had more room for social interplay, recreation and artistic activities such as dance, drawing and story-telling. This was partly due to their wants and needs being less and partly due to their good attunement with the world around them meaning less than half of their day was pre-occupied with satisfying such needs. Their effectiveness in optimising their lifestyle came through a deep empathy for, and resonance with, their social and natural context. It is telling that depression is seldom found within indigenous cultures yet of epidemic proportions in Western culture.[4]

There is a particular Western point of view that the reason indigenous peoples have not developed technologically like the West is because of a lack of intelligence. However, others hold the view that these traditional cultures did not develop like the West because the desire was not there. They lived lives that were attuned to their environment with plenty of social time; they did not perceive the need to advance through technology, as their activities were not perceived as work that needed to be efficiently (yet ultimately unsustainably) enhanced; their 'work' was an enjoyable aspect of life. With this perspective one could view indigenous cultures as having evolved in a deeper way through attitude and psyche – a 'cultural individuation' – where the individual and community individuate in-tune with the dynamics of their reality. By contrast, Western culture could be viewed as having evolved in a more egotistic way so the individual and the collective individuation process is left wanting, in turn feeding the ego's anxious need for yet more grasping desire. That said, we ought not to delude ourselves that pre-civilised life in the West was all sweet harmony and the insights indigenous wisdom provide us do need to be tempered with evidence of dysfunctional social relations in indigenous tribes; the studies of the Nuer and Dinka tribes of South Sudan, for instance. Evidence of social problems within indigenous cultures is by no means rare and it would be naïve to assume the same for Palaeolithic and Neolithic indigenous European cultures. Yet, there is wisdom inherent in these ancient cultures, which can be applied to the challenges in our midst. As anthropologist Stanley Diamond says, it is not a case of hankering after some paradise-lost but rather of realising the contradictions and possibilities for integration between indigenous cultures and civilised ones as a way of helping understand and deal with our present predicament.[5] And neuroscientist Iain McGilchrist points out:

> We might have to revise the superior assumption that we understand the world better than our ancestors and adopt a more realistic view that we just see it differently – and may indeed be seeing less than they did.[6]

Embedded participation

Cultural ecologist David Abram notes that many indigenous people know their surroundings so intensely that they are sensitive to its private presence, taking care not to offend it, much like Westerns take care not to offend other people in their company. This participatory relation with Nature is deeply embedded into their culture and psyche. To inflict unnecessary harm on Nature is to inflict harm on one's own life and family, a grave act. From this deep understanding, a kinship of reciprocal respect develops which makes for a culture of reverence.[7] Rather than life being seen as something to be controlled, it is understood as something to be communed with; we learn to participate in a conversation with life, an improvisational dance.[8] There is a qualitative difference within the community of Nature, a distinctness – say between other animals, plant and humans – and yet not a separateness. This distinctness recognises our unique specialities while communing within a diverse community.[9] It is a stepping back from the immediacy of life which humans undertake.[10] In this regard, kinship is not a homogenous union in an undifferentiated way, but a respectful kinship of *comm-union* within diversity where humans are recognised as creatures of distance with the ability to re-present reality and so differentiate with it. This differentiation and distancing can enhance our meaningfulness of relationship with the world we distance from rather than de-sacralise or overly abstract it, stripping it of meaning and purpose.[11] This ability to step back, rationalise and re-present makes it all the more necessary for humans to maintain a healthy, permeable human-Nature relation, as otherwise we easily become deluded and diseased by our own extraction through abstraction.

The cosmic rhythm

Archaeologists researching the sites of the Caral peoples of ancient Peru found no weapons, only hundreds of musical instruments such as tone flutes. It would seem that their over-arching cultural goal was one of nourishing life through music – the ancient art of elevating vibrations to enhance the resonance reverberating throughout Nature.[12] Seeing themselves as caretakers of this world, they connected with the sacred rhythm of the cosmos and sought to help nourish it.[13] A descendant of these Peruvian people is Arkan Lushwala who, in his beautiful book *The Time of The Jaguar,* warns us, 'if we do not listen to the cosmic rhythm, we trip and fall'.[14] Perhaps Steve Taylor's 'fall' in the West, due to an egotistic way of attending to life, is a cultural tuning-out from the cosmic rhythm, turning a blind eye, deaf ear and closed heart to the divine Music of Nature.

We have seen how in ancient Europe a patriarchal, dominator approach took over from an equalitarian, partnership culture. We have explored how the underlying cultural assumption for modern Western society became a sense of separation from Nature – what Bateson calls the original corruption – which breeds a competitive dog-eat-dog world where one either dominates or becomes dominated. We have also seen how certain traits have a habit of reinforcing themselves and so perpetuate the prevailing perception of reality: a sense of separation from Nature encourages a split in psyche, which enhances anxiety, which feeds the ego, which exacerbates our sense of separation. So how do we break out of this vicious cycle? As writer Mary Jane Zimmerman suggests:

> We live in an exciting time, where the interaction between different cultures has the potential to bring all of us into more consciousness about how we both structure and take in reality. We also live in a perilous time, a time which needs this new level of cultural self-awareness in order to survive. Thus the dialogue between cultures is crucial and it is especially important that the dominant culture begins to listen more humbly and respectfully to those cultures which still embody the relational ways of knowing which have atrophied in the West.[15]

Wildness

In Wildness is the preservation of the world.
Henry David Thoreau[16]

The root meaning of wildness is being wilful or uncontrollable.[17] It is an expression of self-will beyond oppression, unfolding in myriad ways, unconfined and ultimately unpredictable. Life is inherently wild. And yet in our paradoxical quest for simultaneous security and freedom, we have sought both to control and wall out this wildness – this 'sea of troubles'. Our rational abstraction of reality defines, boxes-up, and confines within an unnatural order of its own making in an attempt to organise and control. As part of this civilising process we grasp for predictability by decontextualising and domesticating life. We remove the essence of wildness from life in order to tame it. The wildness of our own psyche becomes suppressed at great angst to ourselves and the rest of life. We overlook the insight this wildness brings and so confine our true, naturally creative and empathic selves. Within the apparent chaos of wildness is a profound beauty and coherence, which is far removed from the 'anarchistic free-for-all' that some of us fearfully imagine; there is a co-creative evolutionary dance of vibrant diversity. As the writer Jay Griffiths poetically says, 'The wild. I have drunk it, deep and raw, and heard its primal, unforgettable roar. We know it in ourselves, for we are wild to the core.'[18] It is within and through wildness that natural truth metamorphoses into an ever-folding and unfolding deeper manifestation. This wildness we should celebrate not denigrate. It should be danced with, not caged.

Ecopsychologist Nick Totton points out that the wild is far from some abandonment, rather it is a place where things learn to relate, tending towards increasing ecological richness.[19] In his book *Wild Therapy*, Totton explains:

> Domestication enriches our lives in countless ways; it is the fabric from which all civilisations so far have been woven. But without a living connection to underlying wildness, domestication is destructive of both human and other-than-human; it operates by eliminating complexity and substituting a crude and simplified replica of wild organisation.[20]

Excessive domestication colonises our own psyche by erecting fences of separation in the all-consuming quest for control. These fences hinder our ability to relate in fully authentic ways and create phobias that repress our wild, intuitive spontaneity. In attempting to control this wildness, our egos create a suppressed shadow which, paradoxically, comes back to haunt us. Totton comments:

... any radical change in our behaviour toward the rest of the wild world depends upon making friends with our own wilderness inside. Until then we are Toad of Toad Hall, egos posturing in the mirror and trying to ignore the Wild Wood.[21]

It's true that a materialist scientific outlook, with its defining atomism and rigid framing, has brought great strides in technological advancement, but who knows how much more – it need not be less – could have been possible if we had stayed truthful to Nature? There is much to learn from Nature's wildness as indigenous wisdom shows us. We need, at long last, to allow the wildness back into our way of understanding, because logic devoid of wildness is crudely simplistic and a refuge for ignorance and needless conflict. As Catherine Keller notes, 'In the wild waters of the world, the fish does not go under. It is in its element. Amidst the unpredictable it swims in grace.'[22]

14. Crossing the Threshold

[A] mood of universal destruction and renewal ... has set its mark on our age. This mood makes itself felt everywhere, politically, socially, and philosophically. We are living in what the Greeks called Kairos – the right moment – for a 'metamorphosis of the gods', of the fundamental principles and symbols. This peculiarity of our time, which is certainly not of our conscious choosing, is the expression of the unconscious man within us who is changing. Coming generations will have to take account of this momentous transformation if humanity is not to destroy itself through the might of its own technology and science ... So much is at stake and so much depends on the psychological constitution of modern man ... Does the individual know that he is the makeweight that tips the scales?

Carl Jung[1]

The call for transformational change

The indigenous elders of Peru explain the complete cycle of humanity as going through three movements: time of creation, time of conservation, time of renewal.[2] The big change happens in the time of renewal which the wise elders say is upon us now. Fundamental to this is a radical change in perception – a shift in conscious awareness – which affects how we attend to life, how we *be, do* and *become*. This time of renewal in which we find ourselves can be very upsetting and painful while also profoundly liberating as we free ourselves from old mental constructs, regulations and habits that keep us imprisoned in the status quo. It is our heartfelt courageous will that moves us towards this liberation through transformation. As we open ourselves up to experiencing life beyond past judgements and preconditions, the energy of transformation flows through us stronger, further encouraging us to open up to the unfolding way ahead even though it is uncertain and unknown. The more we embrace new ways of perceiving, attending and operating, the more we allow the birth of new experiences, new creations and new beginnings to sprout forth. The death of old habits provides for a creative time of birthing and nurturing. This time of renewal is the time to allow new springs of civilisation to flow.

The threshold from death to rebirth that individuals, organisations and communities need to cross can seem like a scary chasm especially when we are all too engrossed in frantically patching up the current way of doing things to meet the ever-rising bills and debts. There is inherent inertia in crossing the threshold. Our feelings of security in the known and sense of safety in numbers by staying in the herd keep us fearfully clinging to old ways. As Bertrand Russell pointed out, 'Collective fear stimulates herd instinct, and tends to produce ferocity toward those who are not regarded as members of the herd.'[3] It reminds me of the line from Morpheus in the film *The Matrix,* 'You have to understand, most people are not ready to be unplugged and many of them are so inured, so hopelessly dependent on the system, that they will fight to protect it.' It is easy to become inured and institutionalised by the status quo.

A paradigm shift

Thomas Kuhn in the early 1960s coined the term 'paradigm shift' when exploring seismic shifts in understanding and found they occur in discontinuous, revolutionary breaks most dramatic after periods of relative stability within a paradigm.[4] Such shifts are a healthy phase in the development of our understanding of reality. Ways of viewing the world are upgraded by bursting beyond the inertia enveloping an outdated construct. We know an era is ending and a new one being conceived when the fundamental assumptions and illusions of the old worldview are exhausted by their inability to deal with the challenges of the day. Economist Joseph Gustav Speth argues, in his book *The Bridge At The End of The World* that today's challenges require nothing less than a revolution in consciousness to a new worldview. He says, 'Today's dominant worldview is simply too biased towards anthropocentrism, materialism, egocentrism, contempocentrism, reductionism, rationalism, and nationalism to sustain the changes needed.'[5] Speth points to a transformation in our midst, 'From materialism, consumerism, getting, the primacy of possessions, and limitless hedonism to personal and family relationships, leisure play, experiencing nature, spirituality, giving, and living within limit.'[6] He warns us:

> Proposals for transformational change will be derided and, when they gain traction, resisted at every turn. It is true but easy to say that the resistance will come from entrenched interests. It will also come from ourselves. We are the consumers and the employees, and we are easily seduced.[7]

Deep and complex influences within our own psyche, our collective consciousness and in the structures pervading our culture are being challenged to radically reshape; at its heart the paradigm shift challenges the very way we view the world and ourselves as embodied within it. One Western trait in desperate need of transformation is our relationship with death (and so life) itself.

The vitality of death

In Nature everything is continually transforming as one stage comes to an end another begins; spirals of death and rebirth, of withdrawing and bursting forth – this is the way of life. The only certainty is uncertainty. Change is what allows for becoming more than we are. It is this humbling mystery of Nature that enchants us in our open-ended quest for the unfolding truth. Contrary to cultural conditioning, life is not about attempting to enforce stability, continuity and the prevention of death, it is about engaging with transformative change of which death is most vital. Life plays with the limitations death brings to yield life. Life without death would lose all significance. Seen in this way, death is the crucible from which the diversity of life metamorphs. And so death forms and transforms the diversity of life. To define death in a singular way without recognising its intrinsic quality within the spiral of life is to try and rationalise something that is beyond rationalising. In the words of David Bohm, 'Everything is alive; what we call "death" is an abstraction'.[8] Exit and re-entry, expiration and inspiration, breakdown and breakthrough, reconfiguration and renewal; the death of galaxies provides for the birth of new constellations; the carbon cycle of photosynthesis and respiration a recycling of life and death through consumption, decomposition and redistribution. Creativity dances between death and rebirth; it surfs the wave on the edge of chaos. Imagine life without death – gridlock. Life would literally suffocate itself without the helping hand of death and rebirth. Just as the Indian goddess Kali is the Great Mother of birth and new life, she is also the great destroyer.[9] By coming to terms with death and transformation we open ourselves up to the truth of life, we free ourselves from the fear of death, allowing ourselves to love each moment, each twist and turn, each high and low, each note and interval.

It is important not to get overly romantic about death nor overlook the infection, decay, pain and grief that goes with it. Yet it is also important for our culture not to shun death. A culture than makes death a taboo fails to comes to terms with the inevitability of change, reconfiguration and rebirth. Excessive fear of transformation and death is egotistic, catalysed by our sense of separation from Nature. A healthy dose of fear, which encourages further probing and understanding before moving forward and exposing oneself to novel situations in life is sensible. Fear becomes unhealthy when it prevents the individual or cultural collective coming to terms with life's transforming thresholds – learning through discomfort and mistakes – where letting go of the safe status quo is essential for embracing the new. Such fear debilitates our exploration and stunts our learning and evolution.

> *And I know one thing.*
> *We are not born to avoid dying by lying low and playing safe.*
> *We are born to live.*
> *We are born to leave the garden more beautiful than we found it.*
> Tim Macartney[10]

Leading across the threshold

Times of impending destruction and creative reconstruction inevitably invoke fear. It takes real leadership to transform in such volatile times – the root of the word leadership is *leith* which means 'to go forth and cross the threshold', to die and be reborn.

Dr Otto Scharmer, Senior Lecturer at MIT, in his *Theory U,* explores how leadership itself needs to transform in order to be able to lead us across this threshold.[11] Leadership, he finds, is about facilitating the process of letting go of old ways and allowing the new to take root. Leaders first transform themselves and then guide and coach others, creating a safe passage for them to cross their own thresholds. Vital to this leadership is a healthy foundation to ground the transformation in, what Scharmer refers to as the soil of the being (the psyche of the individual) and the soil of the organisation (the culture of the organisation). It is this soil that allows the old ways to die and yield nutrients for new growth at a personal and organisational level; much like healthy soil breaks down decaying matter to provide vital nutrients for new growth. The soil of us is our inner being, this is where we can start to envision the future on the other side of the chasm and so contemplate crossing the threshold. Interestingly, the word 'human' comes from the Latin *humus* meaning soil or earth, the same origin as 'humility'. Likewise, the 'Adam' of Genesis originates from *adama,* a Hebrew noun meaning soil.[12] We remain humble with our feet on the ground, and our psyche attuned in Nature. Many of today's leaders, such as Paul Polman CEO of Unilever, are now pointing to humility as an important attribute of leading with integrity.[13]

We can picture our encapsulated egos, like encapsulated seeds, which open up through permeability within the soil of our unconscious psyche and surrounding neighbourhood. By sending roots out into the soil, transformation from encapsulation to germination unfolds; our sense of separation dissipates with this nourishing receptivity.[14] As we transform, we explore new inner and outer possibilities, embracing virgin experiences in a spiralling, pulsating ebbing and flowing of learning through becoming. Our ego-self is ever-ready to bring us back out of the heart if the fear becomes too much for our courage. It may feel like a continual tussle, even a battle in the early stages of this transformation as we explore our self-Self attunement. Through practice, we become more adept at thinking and feeling with the intuitive bodymind (heart entrainment with brain, gut and all sensory organs).

In transforming, we become pioneers on our own journey of individuation, while gaining experience which can be useful for others wishing to embark on their own journey. For Nan Huai Chin, a Zen

Buddhist Master, Taoist Master and Confucian scholar, the seven steps towards being a great leader are actually seven places: awareness, stopping, calmness, stillness, peace, true thinking, attainment.[15] Courage-based leading allows for these places to be found within the individual and collective learning environment. This is emergent leadership that recognises the vitality of co-innovating new ways of operating beyond the confines of predefined outcomes.

Fear-based leading	Courage-based leading
Authoritarian	Emancipation
Leader-follower relation	Co-creative relation
Motivated by power	Motivated by love
Blame culture	Compassionate culture
Risk-averse	Pioneering
Adversarial	Inspirational
Competitive	Empathic
Command and control	Improvisational

We can *encourage* and accompany others through sharing our experiences. Likewise others can encourage and accompany us as new possibilities are encountered. In accompanying others in their learning quest into deeper awareness and understanding, we question and converse. After all, we *Homo sapiens* are primarily social creatures. This sharing of feelings and findings is immensely important and enriching for everyone involved. This is an inspirational and improvisational kind of facilitating. It encourages a meeting of minds through an appreciation both of what we have in common and of how our differences serve to complement our co-learning.

This inspirational facilitation provides safety and freedom – amidst the volatility and uncertainty – to question and share concerns, anxiety, motivations and experiential learning. A willingness to invite questioning of all kinds of assumptions and beliefs allows an opening up for new ways of thinking, listening and sharing. 'Leaders' in this mould are not leading 'followers'; they are cultivating a co-creative environment where transformation happens. They may have special experience gained through personal pioneering experiences, and yet, with humility and courage, share this with others. In leading they are nurturing an open, receptive, loving environment for individuals and the community to tap into as they move forward in engaging fresh possibilities. In this way, preconditions, past-experiences, expectations and judgments can be aired and shared, allowed to either dissipate or transmute into learning. Likewise, leaders of this mettle are open to temporarily relinquishing, rotating, or taking a step back from, leadership when circumstances dictate.

By its very nature, this kind of co-creative leading is neither hierarchical nor subservient nor adversarial. There is no 'enemy' to fight, mountain to conquer or power to manipulate; yet there is fear, trepidation, passion, courage, suffering, empathy, sharing, charisma and encouragement. It is less about orchestrating or conducting and more about facilitating the ability of others to attune themselves. The result is more effective, resilient teams who are able to face increasing uncertainty with renewed inspiration, creativity and love. This kind of leading recognises the vulnerability, needfulness and co-creative potential of each person. The leader makes mistakes; in so doing opening up to further becoming. Correspondingly, leading entails *pioneering* (adventurously exploring new possibilities), *prototyping* (continual questioning, testing, letting-go and questing forward), *guiding* (passing the benefit of one's learning experience on to others along with intuitive insight and a keen eye for hazards and possible breakthroughs, much like a Sherpa guide), and *accompanying* (being alongside others as co-learners, assisting and encouraging an open receptivity in both the individual and collective space). Above all, it entails listening, sharing and leading from the heart. As Anne Dillard notes, 'Good leadership comes from people who have penetrated their own inner darkness and arrived at the place where we are at one with one another.'[16]

Part Three:

Seeing Beyond

15. The Communion of Opposing Tensions

When male and female combine,
All things achieve harmony.

Lao Tzu[1]

Harmony

Vital to life is the dynamic communion of differing relationships – a reciprocating synergistic energy that impels organic growth. This is what György Doczi refers to as 'dinergy' (his own word created by combining the Greek *dia* – meaning 'across, through, opposing' – and 'energy').[2] In other words integration and differentiation are co-creative. This goes directly to the root of one of life's paradoxes concerning why at every turn we find opposing tensions – the yin and yang of life. The creative communion between these seemingly opposing forces is what induces growth and breathes life.[3] As the writer Reshad Feild notes, 'This world requires the creative tension of opposites, and it is here we can see the miracle of multiplicity. Unity is not the miracle; the miracle is in the diversity.'[4]

For Doczi, harmony is a dinergistic relationship where different contrasting elements complement through a merging or joining. The word 'harmony' has its root in the Greek *harmonia* meaning 'to fit together'. Diverse influences integrate in a way that creates the harmonious 'music of life' – a pleasant attunement of differences.[5] The rhythm and resonance these harmonising tensions invoke the experience of beauty within us.[6] The tension is not just between each note, but also between a note and the silence permeating through it. Creative energy attunes with the stillness in its midst; content in dinergic relation within context. This reciprocity of content relating within context is the way of life and it is through our presencing of the moment that we can embrace this primal creative tension of opposites.

Doczi insightfully recognises that it is the limits within Nature – the boundaries or thresholds – which allow for these reciprocating combinations to create. As Hunter Lovins put it, 'Nature uses limits as the crucible within which it creates.'[7] It is what Doczi calls the 'power of limits' – the force behind creation. In sharing one's limitations with another we complement each other, in turn creating diversity, which breeds and supports more life.[8] In other words, limitations are both restrictive and creative. Operating within restraints, Nature creates limitless varieties – from thresholds comes creativity, from restrictions comes diversity. And so we can understand that the creation of life's beauty is through the dynamic communion of reciprocal influences powered by limits. It is life's challenges that provide the opportunities for us to develop, diversify and become more than we are. Rather than tension fuelling our anxiety, egotism and sense of separation (which only exacerbates opposite-mindedness), by opening our conscious awareness to the receptive presence in our midst we allow the energetic tensions of life to enrich us.

The dance of Yin and Yang

Ancient Chinese physicians studied these seemingly opposing forces in Nature. They called them yin and yang – the soft and the hard, the shadow and the light, the negative and the positive, the receptive and the responsive, the feminine and the masculine. By attuning the tensions of these yin and yang qualities of life one achieves rejuvenation and harmony. Just as *dia* means between or through boundaries, it is the relationship between or through these tensions of yin and yang that makes for our reality. There is no either/or, rather there is only the challenge/opportunity to find the right harmonic within and through the tension. In certain life situations a little more yang than yin may be useful, in others a little more yin than yang – much like with the twisting and turning primordial spiral as it attunes. It is only when one side of the reciprocal relationship

> side of the reciprocal relationship begins to dominate and
> so undermines the reciprocity of the dinergic relationship
> that *dis-harmony* or *dis-ease* ensues. East and West, yin and
> yang, masculine and feminine, rational mind and intuitive
> heart are not in dualistic competition, but rather in dinergic
> reciprocation.

Communion

Tantra is an ancient tradition of the aboriginal tribes of India some
3,000 BC, before the Aryan invasions that led to the formation
of Vedic and Brahmanical India.[9] For Tantra, consciousness is a
fundamental property of the universe, permeating within every sub-
atomic vibration and nested at all scales of mind within an over-
arching Creative Intellect. Tantra is essentially about expanding
one's awareness by becoming conscious of the cosmic aspects of
life.[10] The consciously attuned reciprocal relation of the ego-self
and true Self is the goal of Tantra. Our dinergic attunement of
conscious mind and unconscious psyche, physical and metaphysical,
yin receptive qualities and yang responsive qualities, can all be
symbolised by the communion of the Shakti sacred feminine and the
Shiva sacred masculine.[11] Conscious attunement through the Shiva-
Shakti communion brings us into the divine awareness of ultimate
reality. Tantra perceives Shakti as the underlying matrix or womb
of all creation and Shiva as our conscious awareness. And so, once
again, we find that it is the attunement of our conscious awareness
within the all-pervasive Mother Nature in our midst that allows for
this awareness.

The old Anglo-Saxon word *wicca* means 'to mould' which is
the origin of the word 'witch' who was someone who infused their
life with magic by moulding the cosmic energies. According to
Tantra specialist André Van Lysebeth, witchcraft, shamanism and
Tantra all share the same indigenous roots in what is called the
Old Religion: the worship of the Goddess and God. This Goddess
and God can be found deep within our psyche as we attune
with Nature.[12] Witchcraft, shamanism, Tantra and other ancient
traditions all explore attunement with the cosmic rhythms of Nature

by embracing the abysmal cosmic presence of the Goddess deep within the wellsprings of our soul. This shamanic way of attending crosses the threshold of self-other and human-Nature through a thinning of perceptual boundaries and a heightening of receptivity to realms beyond the ego. It is what David Abram calls a primordial participatory mode of perception.[13] In the Judaic mysticism of Kabbalah we find that the human becomes One when he/she unifies with Shekinah, the Feminine Divine Presence also referred to as Motherly Space or Divine Ground of all being. Likewise in ancient Indian Samkhya philosophy, Akasha is the dynamic space or cosmic womb, and in the ancient Chinese tradition of Taoism, the Tao is the Mysterious Female from which all of creation flows, the ground of Heaven and Earth. In all these ancient traditions, the fully realised being is one who knows the masculine yet is grounded in the feminine. The sacred feminine is the soil of our soul; to create a sense of separation from it is to corrupt our conscious way of attending.

Carl Jung explored the contra-sexual anima and animus forces and emphasised the feminine oceanic presence of our unconscious giving birth to the conscious ego-self which has to remain rooted in this presence during its journey of self-realisation. And yet in the West this has not happened; as we have explored, our rationalising ego-consciousness has alienated itself from its own Mother. The communion of the psychical reciprocating relationships has been severed. As Arkan Lushwala says:

> In the world ruled by the conquerors with their great enterprises, there is no place for listening to the commands of the heart or to follow the mysterious motion of the feminine principle. Everything has to be controlled, quantified and calculated from the head so that results are achieved and there are no undesirable surprises. Feminine intelligence has become less important and the voice of the feminine is not being heard.[14]

Yet, many in the West are conscious of an epochal shift, whereby the opposing tensions of the masculine and feminine commune for a deeper perception of reality beyond illusion. Every human has both masculine and feminine qualities within them either lying dormant, suppressed or actively embodied. It is part of our own journey of self-realisation to embody these sacred masculine and feminine qualities. The sacred masculine energies are not ones of domination and control – these are the egotistic traits of the un-individuated masculine. Sacred masculine traits are spontaneity, creativity, strength, passionate conviction, energetic responsiveness and rational logic. These qualities counterbalance the sacred feminine qualities of fluidity, receptivity, shape-changing metamorphosis, empathy and intuitive reasoning.[15] There is no need to wrestle with and control the Feminine through rational logic and reductionist science but rather to dance with Her by letting go of control, allowing the dance to find its natural rhythm of space (feminine) and notes (masculine). Each is within the other and each needs the other for deeper realisation – this is the unfolding dance of life.

Ripe for metamorphosis

As we have explored in Part Two, in recognising the illusion of separation we can start to become conscious of it and so perceive beyond. This comes with a profound shift – a metamorphosis – in our conscious awareness. This metamorphosis is not so much a dissolving of the ego as a conscious embodiment of it within the divine presence of Nature whereupon it opens its permeability to the deeper unconscious soul-scape. As the ego starts to untangle, rarefy and soften, the illusion starts to be robbed of its conscious energy.

Hence, our life challenge becomes our continual return to the wellspring – the Eye of the Heart. The urge to control or confront dissipates. Rather than becoming defensive or aggressive in the face of malevolence, we recognise that in providing no opposition through humility the malevolence dissipates by itself. We master not by conquering but by attuning. We do not need to try and force certain outcomes or dominate particular events. As soon as we try and manipulate or control, our heart entrainment is upset as our ego comes out of attunement with our soul. We learn – through practice, patience and dedication – that our soul attuned within the World Soul becomes the source of all authentic movement. In fact, it always has been it is just that we are becoming consciously aware of it as we gain direct perception of each unfolding moment. This awareness (and the more we bring it into our presence the easier it becomes) can start to flow through all our daily interactions. This is the 'action through non-action' that Tao philosophy speaks of. As Cynthia Bourgeault describes it:

> When ... the vibrational field of a particular human heart comes into spontaneous resonance with the divine heart itself, then finite and infinite become a single, continuous wavelength, and authentic communion becomes possible.[16]

The continual challenge is to remain grounded and centred as situations unfold, letting go of the outcome while fully accepting the co-creativity each present moment offers us. This is far easier said than done and requires a deep understanding of our self-Self attunement.

16. Natural Inclusion

All of space is full of presence.

John O'Donohue[1]

Natural Inclusion is a ground-breaking way of perceiving reality developed by British scientist and former President of the British Mycological Society, Alan Rayner. At its core is the understanding that everything flows within the natural influence, or natural communion, of everything else. Bodies or beings are different and distinct from their surroundings and yet flow within and through their surroundings.

Space is not empty distance between things, but a limitless intangible receptive ocean, which permeates within, throughout and beyond all tangible form. Space is that presence literally everywhere within which all forms interplay in a co-creative evolutionary dynamic. Everything we perceive as an object or body is made up of space and energy. The energy vibrations are within and through space. There is no separation of the energetic vibrations and space, they include each-in-the-other. Space and energy are distinct yet mutually inclusive presences. Nothing is entirely separate.

This clearly resonates in some ways with the scientific findings of relativity and quantum theory with its concept of an all-pervading QV sea of energy across space. Yet it differs in that the inclusion of energy within space flies in the face of prevailing abstract rationality, which supposes space (as nothing) is separate from matter (as something). This is the Euclidean assumption that rationalistic science is based upon, and what Stephen Harrod Buhner points to when he notes:

> ... our whole culture is based on the illusion that Euclid created with his mathematics. That illusion, which we take to be so very real, actually has little to do with the real world and nothing at all to do with natural environments.[2]

Earlier we mentioned how Euclid in 300 BC founded our Western understanding of space in mathematically defining matter as neat packets located at specific points totally severed from space. We have also explored how our quantum understanding of matter is of it being energetic vibrations of light (electromagnetic energy). Yet for quantum physics, which is influenced by Euclidean geometry, these energetic vibrations are perceived as separate from space. Often quantum physicists talk of 'strings' or 'wavicles' of vibrating energy being 99.99% space and a miniscule fragment of matter which is deemed separate from space. This separation is vital for abstract mathematical assumptions underpinning theoretical notions of space, energy and matter within Western rationalistic science. Yet the separation of space and matter, which most of us in the West take as reality, is an assumption of convenience, an abstraction of content from context at the most fundamental level.

This may be confusing for our minds to grasp, and it isn't easy to explain through the written word, so an example may help here. Picture a leaf. As we have explored, all of Nature exhibits semi-permeability. The leaf is in continual attunement with its natural surroundings to greater or lesser degrees (even if it is fallen from the tree, decaying on the ground). The leaf's surface is covered in pores which exchange oxygen, carbon dioxide and water vapour with its surroundings. Within the leaf are millions of cells all relating with each other in much the same way through semi-permeable membranes continually exchanging. Picture one cell within the leaf, not only is its membrane semi-permeable but all the molecules, atoms, subatomic particles (or wavicles) and everything within its structure is semi-permeable. In fact, the closer we look, we see that all these wavicles are vibrations of light humming away within space. From a Natural Inclusion perspective these vibrations of light are not actually separate from space they are included within space. The vibrations (which make up the appearance of mass to us) are 100% space plus energy. There is no separation; separation is an abstraction created by our rational minds to help us grasp, yet in so doing, fragment reality. The peculiar position quantum physics finds itself in, of seemingly less and less matter and more and more space, is transcended as soon as the space-matter dualism is transcended. Energy contains space within it, never to be separated. Everything is *dynamically distinct* as local identities, not *definitively discrete* as autonomous entities.

The key themes of Natural Inclusion

The formulation of Western rationalistic science is founded upon the assumption that matter is separate from space. Tangible form is split from intangible presence, the material split from the immaterial. Natural Inclusion undoes this corruption.

The abstract separation of content from context extracts our attention from being embodied within Nature into objectified fragments, in so doing severing our conscious awareness from its natural source of vitality. Natural Inclusion cleanses this abstraction through a re-immersion back into Nature.

The reconciliation of Western dualisms (space and matter, light and dark, masculine and feminine, life and death) transforms our way of attending from the divorced estrangement of content from context into the sacred communion or 'remarrying' of reality.

In perceiving the world as a participle, a marrying of noun (to be) and verb (to do), reality is viewed as a process of becoming, a participation. Natural Inclusion is a dynamic logic of reality rather than the static logic of mechanistic reductionism. As human 'becomings' we are no longer 'parts' of Nature but dynamic expressions within Nature. We are flowing, attuning vibrating participations within life rather than separate 'objects' or 'subjects'.

In opening up to and fully experiencing Nature in its breath-taking, awe-inspiring process of becoming, we release ourselves from the suffocating confinements of abstract rational logic. We become inspired by the co-creativity all around us. In attuning with Nature we co-inspire the evolution of life.

An each-in-the-other awareness, much like the empathic reverence of indigenous cultures, releases us of the dominating need for control-based thinking and dog-eat-dog competition.

Receptivity and responsiveness

Quantum theory has helped the rational mind dispel the myth that space is a physical absence (nothing) and matter is a physical presence (something). This dualism of space-matter as absence/presence is not how reality really is. As Natural Inclusion explores, space is not only a real and primal presence but one that is utterly vital to the very possibility of the existence and movement of living form. Yet words used conventionally to define 'things' and 'actions' struggle adequately to represent such a primary, all-pervasive influence in our cosmos. The words 'void' or 'quantum vacuum' (QV) go some way in attempting to describe this truly infinite influence. But perhaps 'receptive presence' is more adequate, in that it depicts space as a continuous ocean – a cosmic womb – that invites energy into manifesting material form rather like a brandy glass beckons spirit into swirling inside and around its hollow interior. Space can be perceived as the conveyor of, not barrier to, natural energy flow. Instead of separation there is inclusion. Space is the Divine Ground, Mother Goddess, Akasha, Shakti, the eternal OM or Divine Darkness; a pregnant presence within which energy spawns.

Radiant energy, or light, can hence be viewed as a 'responsive presence' that is drawn into circulation around local centres of space – like spiralling vortices or chakras – within a continuum of space everywhere; energy 'becomes' dynamic bodily form within the 'being' of space. Put another way, space is the receptive presence from which energy projects its responsiveness; together they co-create a receptive-responsive dynamic of energy within space. Rather like yin and yang, space and energy need each other to manifest their complementary qualities, engaging each other, no one without other. The receptive yin is invitingly spacious and the responsive yang is movingly energetic. There is a continual flux of receptivity and responsiveness much like a continual breathing in and out. So we see that everything in reality, from social relationships to brick walls, is manifested as unique blends of space-energy, each exhibiting unique vibrational resonance – recall Haisch's snowflakes of unique form yet originating from beyond form. Rayner calls these space-energy blends 'flow-forms'. For Rayner, we inhabit Nature as flow-forms in a limitless pool of space, each in the others' influence, not as objects isolated by, and cut apart from, space.

To help with what may seem to be a mind-boggling description of space, energy and reality, try to envisage energy without space. What would it be like? Without space the energy would have no form and so it would be like an infinitely compressed 'dot', rather like our Western view of the cosmos at the moment just prior to the Big Bang. Then try and envisage space without energy. What would that be like? Without energy it would have no flow and so nothing to form. It would be an infinitely open yet empty void, again rather like our Western view of the cosmos just prior to the 'dot' appearing that leads to the Big Bang. In reality both space without energy and energy without space does not actually occur, thank goodness.

Our overly rationalistic mind desires to turn the intangible into the tangible so it can define, abstract, name and categorise 'it'. Yet space is inescapably an intangible, immaterial, receptive presence. As an intuitive, perceptive feeling we can perhaps get closer to an understanding of space by saying that 'being' is spatial and 'becoming' is energetic; that way we sense and feel the divergent yet convergent difference of space and energy as receptive presence and responsive presence. It is this dinergic co-creation of receptivity and responsiveness which manifests flow-forms as yin-yang configurations of space-energy. Nothing is isolated as everything is an energetic configuration of-and-in intangible space. Hence, 'self' is not independent from 'other'; rather there is always a degree of energetic engagement of each-in-the-other. Instead of rationally abstracting something out of the context of its natural neighbourhood in order to understand it, we empathise with it in a relaxed yet actively engaged way – a dynamic 'open receptivity' within reality rather than a grasping objective extraction from it. Space is no longer viewed as meaningless or empty but a womb or ocean or vibrant expanse full of creative potential. As Abram explains, 'Space is no longer experienced as a homogenous void, but reveals itself as this vast and richly textured field in which we are corporeally immersed.'[3] Space can therefore be perceived as a silent yet vibrant pulsating field of vitality. Energy emerges as a primordial birthing from the pregnant darkness of this cosmic ground.

The dual notions of a receptive presence and creative energetic urge influence the birth, growth and transformation of all natural flow-forms. These notions resonate with areas of contemporary theology, for instance: panentheism (God as the receptive-creative presence of Nature); Taoism (the receptive presence of the Tao and creative energy of *chi);* Sufi mysticism (the soulful receptive presence of the Divine as the origin of life, and Spirit as the spark of life); Celtic-Druid spirituality (the all-pervasive presence throughout Nature from which the life-spirit *nwyfre* creates). What Natural Inclusion brings is a Western scientific understanding of this receptive-creative presence as space within which energetic flow-forms (as creative energetic configurations) continuously emerge and reconfigure.

Five pointers for Natural Inclusion:[4]

1. Space, as limitless, eternal openness that cannot be cut, pervades matter/energy.
2. Matter/energy cannot exist independently from space, unless confined to an inert, dimensionless point.
3. Regions of space free from detectable matter/energy appear dark and feel intangible to sensors of detectable wavelengths of electromagnetic radiation.
4. All distinguishable (to our senses) form is local-in-nonlocal flow-form, a dynamic inclusion of space and matter/energy.
5. Time cannot exist independently from natural energy flow as a dynamic configuration of space.

The cultural barriers to Natural Inclusion

Mathematical barrier:

Conventional mathematics and geometry is based on discrete, completely definable numerical units. To assume discreteness helps the rational mind define and atomise, yet it abstracts reality into something unnatural. While quantum theory has been grappling with the mathematical concepts of zero and infinity, it still defines infinitesimally small particles – quark strings – as cut-out bits of matter excluded from space. By separating matter from space it can be completely definable (although in an unreal, abstract definition). This allows for the pretence of splitting up the continuous energy flow of reality into sections which can then be reconstituted rather like freeze-framed shots in a film. This 'cutting up' is at the heart of rationalism and provides mathematical convenience yet demeans the creative potential of life.

Cognitive barrier:

In abstracting matter from space, we view matter as something and space as nothingness between. This view encourages us to separate content from context or organism from environment. While holism has sought to overcome some of the loss reductionism brings in breaking down everything into discrete parts, holism still views the parts and the wholes as interconnected bits of matter extracted from space. The relationships between these parts are viewed as energetic linkages or webs. Certainly this interconnectedness helps to counteract the unnatural severance implicit in reductionism, yet struggles to acknowledge the distinct but mutually inclusive natural presences of space and energy. Within Natural Inclusion, content is within context, everything is within and includes the all-pervasive presence of space. Relationships are inter-dependent flow-forms, not interconnected parts. To perceive a part of something is absolutely fine as a scientific endeavour as long as we recognise that we have abstracted it and so need to recontextualise it. In other words, the right-left-right hemispheric way of attending described by McGilchrist and the original participation-separation-final participation of Barfield require the final stage of recontextualisation to bring the abstract content back into its participatory flow-form.

Fear barrier:

The fear of uncertainty and vulnerability in an unpredictable world is what may have catalysed our desire for abstract certainty. Death itself is an abstraction of one phase of life. In recognising the seemingly abysmal void of space not as absence but as receptive presence we may feel able to include rather than separate. We recognise the fluidity of reality where nothing is absolutely isolated and everything is each in the others' influence to varying degrees.

Linguistic barrier:

Abstract rationality provides for either/or definitions of separation while excluding the middle. This provides for neatly packaged nouns and verbs, which serve to reinforce dualism (and monism) to an extent that relational tensions often become twisted into separation. Our view of life becomes adversarial or coercive, with something either in opposition to or forced into union with something else. Natural Inclusion allows us to transcend these linguistic either/or dualities by recognising the interplay of energy within space, each fluidly in the influence of the other.

Co-creative evolution

In Part One we explored how the separation of content from context was a foundational assumption for a Neo-Darwinian view of 'natural selection' as the preservation of favoured races in the struggle for life, where evolutionary success is dependent on the competitive elimination of others. This assumption is rooted in rationalistic logic that compels us to draw an imaginary hard line or discontinuity between 'self' and 'other'. Our prevalent view is of the individual 'self' or organism as an exception from its spatial neighbourhood, separated by a discrete boundary. In reality, it is the variable semi-permeability of an organism's distinguishing boundary – its free permeability to space but variable permeability to energy – which enables it both to be present and to evolve (to 'become'). In other words, the organism co-creates through a participatory relation with its surroundings.

Having extensively studied the natural world, Rayner found that rather than simplifying and helping our understanding of reality, the imposition of discontinuity onto natural continuity corrupts our understanding if it is taken literally as 'complete truth'. As Rayner notes:

We rank and file ourselves as we rank and defile Nature, setting the scene for profound social, psychological and environmental distress even as we glorify in our apparent technological prowess. Everywhere, the one dimensional line is drawn, with discrete numerical points set out like mileposts along it, between 'here' and 'there', 'me' and 'you', 'us' and 'them', 'success' and 'failure', 'winners' and 'losers', 'rich' and 'poor', 'first' and 'last', 'alive' and 'dead', 'ends' and 'means' – with little thought given to the dreadful costs incurred in the wastelands along its margins.[5]

'Natural inclusion' evokes a different attitude towards Nature from 'natural selection'. Organisms can be understood as co-creative and dynamically responsive in an on-going evolutionary flow. This inclusive way of understanding views evolution as participatory where human beings and the world are in empathic reciprocal relationship. The evolutionary diversification of life is a dynamic process of co-creative influence, over vastly differing scales from microcosm to macrocosm. The receptive presence of space is what allows for everything to influence everything else. Rather than hard-lined boundaries we can perceive energetic interfacings between inner and outer localities. It is something that many scientists and practitioners have intuitively felt yet been unable to describe within the confines of Western rationalism.

This way of attending allows a relationship of feeling through space to form along with an attuning resonance between us and the world around us. We start to intuitively feel and perceive the world as it really is – spatially and dynamically continuous – rather than numbed by our own abstraction. This helps us shift from a purely self-centred, power-hungry, manipulative, ego-centric engagement with our world to a more empathic embodiment of our world. Our disposition becomes one of care rather than of control.[6] This can allow for reconciliation with and re-enchantment of Nature. It allows our scientific-philosophy to shift from being inherently competitive and life-damaging, to being compassionate and life-supporting.[7] Gone with the illusion of separation is our carcinogenic way.

Importantly, core to this inclusive worldview is an understanding of the roles and complementary of individual and communal 'needfulness' in evolutionary diversification – as distinct from capitalist self-interest and communist group-interest. What is evolutionarily fitting for each organism (and human) is ultimately fitting for the neighbourhood, because no one can be isolated from the other. Naturally there are limits within the neighbourhood which, as we have explored, act as the crucible for co-creativity. Energy flows are receptive responsive reciprocations, like ebbs and flows of tidal waters or like fish attuning with eddies in a river or like breathing points that reciprocally inspire from and expire to their immediate surroundings. In the words of Rayner:

> Real life does not inhabit an even playing field of energy, space, and time, nor is it governed by a local sovereign power or bureaucracy that prescriptively tells it what to do or judges what it does. Instead it continually both changes and responds to changes in the contextual circumstances of its natural neighbourhood in an improvisational process of autocatalytic flow, which gives rise to evolutionary and ecological complexity and succession. Through this process of natural inclusion, an opening is made dynamically for an extraordinary diversity and complexity of interdependent forms and patterns of life to coevolve over myriad nested temporal and spatial scales. The breath-taking variety that we can find in a crumb of soil, a patch of chalk grassland, a coral reef, or a tropical forest comes into being under the guidance of no more and no less than the responses and contributions of its membership to natural energy flow in a natural 'sustainability of the fitting'.[8]

Neo-Darwinism views evolution as a degenerative process of ever-diminishing competitive options setting ourselves on course for an evolutionary dead-end ruled by selfish ascendance. Yet, from another perspective, evolution is a co-creative process of ever opening possibilities in a transforming spatial context.[9] It is not a battleground of one-way adaptation but a complementarity of local and non-local through mutual attunement. Our perception of evolution breaks free from the abstract rationality of competitive materialism and opens out into the co-creative process of natural inclusion.[10] Sustainability, not supremacy, is the path of evolutionary and ecological continuity.

17. The New Paradigm

In times of turmoil, the danger lies not in the turmoil, but in facing it with yesterday's logic.

Peter Drucker[1]

Yesterday's logic is founded upon the objective exclusivity of rationalism and egotism. It is the logic of control-based thinking that sets humans apart from each other and from the rest of Nature. It is this very logic that is at the heart of all our crises – world poverty, climate change, biodiversity loss, social inequality, and so on. And yet many of today's attempted solutions apply the same flawed logic without stepping back to question it. If we have any hope of rectifying the error of our ways, this logic needs to be put right at its root otherwise all we can hope for is to merely delay the inevitable endgame through efficiency tweaks to an inherently carcinogenic *modus operandi*.

The word 'radical' originates from *radix,* the Latin for 'root'. The paradigm shift now upon us has to go to the root source of our carcinogenic approach and so be radical – philosophically, scientifically, culturally and economically. With this in mind, let's review what we have explored in this book to find some clarity and momentum for moving forward from here:

Philosophy

Philosophy in the West set out with the noble quest for divine illumination through the love of wisdom. Yet, over time (as our way of attending became more narrow-minded) we tended to focus on the manipulation and control of objects isolated from their lived-in context, providing abstract representations of the world. We began to perceive the abstractions as complete truth while increasingly overlooking the flows, connectivity, cohesiveness and intrinsically dynamic nature of reality.

Science

With the advent of the Scientific Revolution, the scientific lens became mechanistic and Nature became de-sacralised. Recent findings in quantum theory challenge some of these materialistic assumptions. Yet the abstract rationality of a hard-line between space and matter is causing us profound problems; it is littering our view of reality with numerous false dichotomies: mind-matter, self-other, human-nature, inner-outer, and so on.

Culture

Culture is greatly influenced by our scientific philosophy and vice versa. Hand-in-hand with our scientific philosophy becoming more inclusive our cultural mindset can become less excessively competitive and more communing, less patriarchal and more reciprocating, less egotistic and more soulful. Narcissism transforms through individuation into compassion; selfishness into service. Our cultural way of attending becomes one of receptive-responsive-reciprocity.

Socio-economics

Social-political-economic models flow from these cultural, scientific and philosophical paradigms. As the paradigms transcend beyond separation into natural inclusion, we find our way in transcending the dualistic either/or tension of capitalist individualism and communist collectivism with participatory social behaviours honouring individual uniqueness within empathic reciprocity.

Education

As Gregory Bateson pointed out, a transformed way of attending can be realised through the processes of education and character formation.[2] Current social-political-economic governance is, in the main, orientated for control. This can, and must, be transformed into education-based methods that inspire rather than suppress our attunement of self-other-Nature. The Latin root for the word 'education' is *educere* meaning to 'bring out' or 'lead forth'. The pioneering British economist E. F. Schumacher recognised that humankind's greatest resource is education and the West's state of crisis may in part have to do with its wrong approach to education.[3] For Schumacher, it is the wisdom that education produces which is paramount; a wisdom which allows each of us to be true to our authentic nature while enhancing the quality of our interrelations, or as Schumacher put it, becoming truly in touch with our centres, where our daily conduct shows a sureness which stems from this inner clarity.[4]

The artisan and the consumer

The medieval word *artificer* or 'maker of art' is where the concept of 'artisan' as a creative maker of art comes from. In Europe, before the advent of industrialisation, art had physical, emotional and spiritual meaning in terms of its contribution to everyday living. Art was the 'right way of making things'.[5] In this artful service of life, the artisan – or craftsman as referred to by social philosopher Richard Sennett, or tradesman as referred to by philosopher and mechanic Matthew Crawford – gains meaningful engagement through the act of creating and delivering something of quality and value to self and society. Sennett views the creative potential for craftsmanship as innate within all of us.[6] The act of doing something well unleashes a deep motivation and sense of wellbeing within the artisan. Through the creative act, the artisan ensures work flows with creative energy and so is a conduit for realising creative potential. Crawford notes that a deep engagement and intrinsic understanding of the task occurs when the artisan dwells in the right way of making things.[7] As philosopher Alexandre Kojeve puts it, the worker is transformed by the work.[8] For Crawford, this is the Homeric interpretation of *Sophia* (the Greek goddess of wisdom), where the head, hands and heart cohere as a fusion of being and doing within the undertaking of purposeful work.[9] Charles Eisenstein in his *Sacred Economics* talks of 'the one who bows into service', recognising the sacred nature of work delivered with loving attention.[10] This is not art for art's sake but craftwork providing value for the consumer. While the consumer pays a fair price for the work, the value to the artisan is beyond the price paid as the sense of meaning the act of creating provides is beyond monetisation. Put another way, the work of the artisan is authentic and beautiful, consisting of an intrinsic richness emanating from a co-creative unfolding process of worker and work which necessarily involves an active engagement of heart, mind, body and soul. It is this transforming nature of wholehearted work that brings coherence and fulfilment, birthing a sense of meaning from which happiness and a rightful sense of place and purpose in society derive. This co-creativity of work and worker is radically different from the enslavement of consumerist capitalism where the commoditisation of creativity is abstracted by the logic of individualistic competition and short-term profit maximisation.

There are still many who make craftsmanship their way of life. In all walks of life people truly care and give their fullest attention to what they provide whether a service provision or a product of consumption, and whether knowledge-based or manual work. Yet, in the Western world, such care and attention is diminishing amidst the contagion of commoditisation.[11] Rampant consumerism marginalises the chances for anyone wishing to make a living doing what they deeply enjoy.

Heart-based living

As Rudolf Steiner noted, 'love is the creative force in the world'.[12] Vital for this paradigmatic transformation is deep attention to how we intuit, feel and think which can be characterised as a shift from fear (denial, separation, insecurity, apathy, over-analysis) to love (empowerment, empathy, encouragement, acceptance, courage, care-taking). Wisdom rooted in love provides the foundation for right thought, emotion and deed. It is what Steiner called 'active, creative thinking' whereby 'head-thinking' is transformed into 'heart-thinking'; such love-infused wisdom is the true basis of all social organisation.[13] A loving interest in each unfolding moment provides for an active creativity which is calm yet energised, patient yet passionate, devoted yet tolerant. Such a moment is given meaning by our immersion in the wellsprings of our heart – our deeper Nature – and can occur regardless of place, whether we find ourselves in an art studio, office, garage, discotheque, forest, or bedroom, for instance. What is primarily important is not 'what' we do, but the 'way' that we do it. Mother Teresa once wisely said, 'We cannot do great things. We can only do small things with great love.'[14] Doing small things with great love transcends the self-limiting illusions of yesterday's logic.

Doc Childre, the founder of *HeartMath,* has explored techniques to help us with heart entrainment in our daily lives, increasing the access to our heart's intuitive guidance and allowing us to become more conscious of our thoughts, feelings and attitude. Simply becoming aware of our beating heart, the space between and through the beats and the rhythm and sensation of our breath can allow our racing mind to slow down, providing an opening for active creativity. It is what Childre calls 'heart-based living'.[15] After all, how we think will determine what we think, see and do.

Nancy Kline, in her book *Time To Think,* explores how every conversation and meeting should become what she calls a 'Thinking Environment' – a way of being where quality of attention, listening, questioning and sharing are paramount. Paying attention without urgency, listening with complete presence; simply treating others as we wish to be treated ourselves. Kline would like every aspect of society to be a Thinking Environment. Whether it be our family relations, schools, organisations or political and governance systems, people should aspire to give deep attention to each other, to really listen without interrupting, to say what they really feel without fear of judgement, to have self-respect and respect for others. This is to live in love, to truly love ourselves and in so doing attend lovingly in all our interrelations.[16]

Co-innovating our future

When discussing our mainstream approach to education, Alan Moore, author of *No Straight Lines,* says that 'we need to move from a process whereby teaching is information delivered by an authority, to one where students are drawn into creating, critiquing and discussing the world we inhabit.'[17] Bring back playtime and group creativity where students brainstorm and playfully engage with real life challenges, learning how to transcend perceived boundaries while tackling the inertia of the status quo. Creativity is the nourishing soil of our society, nurturing transformative solutions for the path ahead. The famous creative John Cleese advocates a rebalancing of our open and closed states of mind (which correspond to McGilchrist's right and left brain hemispheres). For Cleese, we enrich our creative potential by staying in the open, playful state for longer, free from deadlines and distractions. Once we have attained a state of intuitive receptivity then creative solutions arise from deep within our unconscious which, with the closed state of mind of the left hemisphere, we can then define into an activity for our to-do list and so manifest the creative inspiration into action. Increasingly schools and colleges are embracing a more collaborative, creative, contemplative, expressive, artful, participatory approach to learning with marked improvement in attendance, quality of attention and results, as well as a more profound learning experience better equipping the students for a purposeful life ahead.

In their book *Leading from the Emerging Future,* Otto Scharmer and Katrin Kaufer, leadership specialists from MIT and the Presencing Institute, advocate cross-sector hubs that bring together stakeholders from local communities, higher education and business to form spheres of hands-on innovation where conversations and relationships combine the intelligence of head, hands and heart. Such hubs allow for what they refer to as 'consciousness-based action research' blending mindful, heartfelt, improvisational co-innovation.[18] Peer group learning and creative commons can now be readily supported through technology platforms and legal frameworks applicable not just for education but also for business and social change. Charles Eisenstein envisions this new dynamic as, 'decentralized, self-organising, emergent, peer-to-peer, ecologically integrated expressions of political will'.[19] This includes embracing the ancient indigenous way of Council in facilitating spaces where groups can open up to the wisdom of the heart to allow co-creativity through a communal atmosphere of sharing, non-judgment and acceptance. In Council, people sit in a circle and commit to being fully present and really listening to each other from the heart, free from distractions, judgements, opinion forming or preparation of a response. Pippa Bond, a facilitator in the ancient way of Council, notes that, 'Council invites empathy, stillness and honesty'.[20] Council is the practice of love which is applicable to all social interrelations from family discussions to executive board meetings. For indigenous cultures, where collective decisions are regularly made through this circle of shared dialogue, it is acceptance rather than consensus which is all important – where an empathic understanding of the differing views of each and all occurs even if everyone is not in agreement with the final decision. This way resentment does not build up and then corrode the community. Differing opinions are healthy and ought to be celebrated as it is the diverse variety of opinions within a community that provides for the resilience needed for long term viability. This emergent approach to co-innovating our future is radically different from the linearity of pre-defined, quantised, time-bound schedules pervading our organisations today.

Radical democracy is what the political theorist, Jeremy Gilbert, explores as the creative potential of the collective which flourishes through diverse individuality.[21] Gilbert stresses that this is not simply about giving greater diversity of voices a chance to be heard, but also embracing the actual right to take part in decision-making, a collective individuation where individuals collectively acknowledge differences in understanding each other's perspectives, leveraging the tensions for continual emergence of new and better ways forward: democracy as an emergent process of becoming. Here creativity is recognised as both the attribute of the self and of the interrelation with other. In this way our freedom and power is found not through isolating ourselves into self-seeking competitive units of separateness but in immersing ourselves in the sea of interrelations in which we find ourselves. Our empowerment is enriched by our sociality.[22] Tensions and disagreements in life are not just inevitable, they are the lifeblood for dinergies to co-create richer outcomes; they are the power of limits that fuel our evolution.

Nature's wisdom

The good news is that, as we open up to the inner and outer depths of ourselves, each other and Nature, we gain awareness of Nature as a powerful source of inspiration, and begin to realise the answers to our pressing challenges are all around and within us. For instance: the attunement that emerges within flocking and shoaling may provide insight for self-organising community groups; nested cycles of ecological transformation may provide insight for social development; diverse microbial soil communities beneath our feet may provide insight for localisation within globalisation; ecosystem-thinking may provide insight for ecological production processes and waste re-use; Nature's regenerative cycles may provide insight for organisational resilience; deep immersions in Nature may provide psychological insights which aid our self-other-Nature attunement. From bacteria to bees and from Aboriginal Australian communities to the Scottish Highlands we start to uncover gems of truth to share in helping our neighbourhoods become vibrant and life-enhancing.

Much has recently been written about the need not just for new techniques, practices, codes and ethics, but also a 'new way of thinking' one which is more 'ecological'. This ecological thinking is emergent and exploratory while recognising the complexity and dynamism of real life beyond the tidy confines of the prevalent Cartesian paradigm. Such ecological approaches are gaining wider recognition in helping new worldviews embed across different fields such as business transformation, community regeneration, social entrepreneurship, education and sustainability. For instance, in my previous book *The Nature of Business,* I explore how ecological thinking can be applied to enable organisations to redesign for resilience in volatile times. Businesses inspired by Nature are ones that locally attune by encouraging permeability of their business 'membrane' in embracing open innovation and co-creativity across diverse stakeholder 'ecosystems'.[23] Another example of applied ecological thinking is the Regenerative Framework, developed by Pamela Mang and Bill Reed of the Regenesis Group.[24] Regenerative approaches emphasise the importance of shifting from a 'doing less bad' mindset into harmonising with Nature. This calls for an ecological worldview that deeply understands and resonates with Nature in recognising the interrelationships at all levels of organisation. It recognises the need for creating a culture of co-creativity; a living awareness of the dynamic integration of human and non-human systems which reawakens us to a deep attunement of human life immersed within – no longer abstracted from – Nature.[25] As Mang and Reed recognise, this harmonisation of human systems with the dynamic energies of Nature is not for the sole purpose of preservation or restoration but for 'the continual evolution of culture in relationship to the evolution of life'.[26] Other examples of pioneering Nature-inspired education facilitations are: the Mycelium School creating the conditions for holistic learning for business and social change; Wild Wisdom Leadership opening leaders and change agents up to the wisdom of Nature; BCI: Biomimicry for Creative Innovation applying ecological thinking for business transformation; The JUMP! Foundation exploring Nature-inspired experiential learning environments within schools; The Natural Change Foundation delivering Nature-immersion workshops catalysing leadership for sustainability.

In opening ourselves up to the deep wisdom of Nature, we undergo a metamorphosis whereupon our creative and imaginative logic and our rational and analytical logic cohere to enable a humble yet courageous sense of purpose to arise in us – so essential for leading in today's turbulent times. Goethe's 'active seeing' as a phenomenological way of perceiving the aliveness of Nature can be a useful tool in opening ourselves up to the wisdom of Nature. Active seeing – whereupon we contemplate an aspect of Nature, say a leaf, in a receptive way for many minutes – enables our bodymind to embody the metamorphosing quality of Nature. Put another way, by presencing Nature, while resisting our left hemisphere's grasping desire to categorise or define, we increase our permeability within Nature which allows our conscious awareness to perceive Nature's explicit multiplicity of diversity and its implicit dynamic unity. In doing this, we may open ourselves up to the intuitive realisation that diversity *is* dynamic unity.[27] Hence we may reveal the insight that we humans are all expressions within an all-pervasive deeper Nature. Steiner, Wittgenstein, Heidegger, Gadamer and other influential Western philosophers have been profoundly influenced by Goethe's active seeing in recognising how such a phenomenology can liberate us from the restrictive patterns of yesterday's logic. In their book *Holonomics,* authors Simon Robinson and Maria Moraes Robinson have translated Goethe's way of seeing into a framework which can be used by decision-makers in business and beyond to transform linear thinking into a presencing way of attending they call 'holonomic thinking'. This approach, they say, 'while acknowledging the importance of the analytical-logical-symbolic aspect of our minds, fully embraces intuition, feeling and sensing', which is vital for our authentic engagement in the work that lies ahead of us.[28]

Nature's wisdom is readily available to us upon tuning-in; the challenge is remaining open to this sensitive way of perceiving life while going about our daily *busi-ness.* As the Master of Emmanuel College, Cambridge, and former Director-General of the National Trust, Fiona Reynolds notes, 'we have become too distracted from ourselves, lacking time or being unwilling to listen to our inner voices and the lessons Nature can teach us'.[29] The more we attune the more we realise that Nature's wisdom is very far from the centralised, atomised and quantised management-thinking pervading so many of today's organisations whether public or private, for profit or non-profit. The seismic challenges that now face us call for a participatory approach to life for now and all time. Deep respect for ourselves, each other and Nature is not some luxury add-on which can be dispensed with in times of economic downturn, it is foundational to who we truly are; without it we become rudderless, tossed this way and that by inauthentic egotistic whims – distracted, diseased and deluded.

Three R's to help ground our paradigm shift:

1) *Re-designing:* new ways of operating and innovating beyond 'hurting' into 'healing' (shifting from the take/make/waste paradigm to a regenerative approach which nourishes life).

2) *Re-establishing:* reconciling our self-other-Nature relation (attuning our self-Self within the embodiment of our neighbourhood, drawing on, for instance: eco-psychology, phenomenology, co-creative community engagement, leading-from-the-heart, contemplative practices, the way of Council, shamanic practices and deep Nature immersions).

3) *Re-kindling:* igniting ancient wisdom through the inspiration of Nature (enabling organisations, communities and societies not merely to reduce their adverse impact but to flourish in the years ahead by practising wise approaches to life that draw on, for instance: ecological thinking, eco-literacy, permaculture, biomimicry and indigenous wisdom).

The paradigm shift

Antagonistic	→	Participatory
Narcissistic	→	Empathic
Materialistic	→	Soulful
Ego as master	→	Ego as assistant
Dominator	→	Partner
Patriarchy	→	Reciprocity
Separation	→	Inclusion

Our primary and ultimate goal has to be to found any new society upon a culture of attunement where we collectively and individually nurture each and everyone's journey of self-Self individuation, self-other reciprocity and human-Nature receptivity. The former Archbishop of Canterbury, Rowan Williams, explains this tuning into the wisdom around and within us as a sacred vision of the world, an attitude of reverence involving 'attention, attunement and atonement'. He says that through our joyful attunement of our intelligent body and intelligent environment, we can restore a life-giving sense of the holy.[30] As William Blake recognised, 'Everything that lives is holy' and through our attunement with what *is* in this present moment of life we realise this holiness.[31] This is our beginning. From here we can breathe into the new paradigm so that we can become all that we truly are in this enchanting and deeply wise world. Our philosophy becomes the conscious awareness of Nature as the wellspring of wisdom. Our scientific endeavours become inspired by and in harmony with Nature. Our culture becomes co-creative and communal without forsaking our uniqueness.

18. The Awakening

Most often one is merely 'outside' experience – things happen to one. One is 'inside' when one ponders over all experience, over the very stuff of life, and to that extent becomes an instrument of truth. At this point the duo of 'outside-inside' becomes redundant.

K. Khosa[1]

Our bodymind boundaries have their job to do in finding the right balance of opening up, while also filtering out. The more porous the boundary, the more receptive we can be and so the more engaged with – yet more exposed to – our neighbourhood. The less porous the boundary, the more protected we can be – yet less engaged with – our neighbourhood. Finding the right level of openness for the situation we are in requires continual attunement. Within our Western paradigm we find ourselves embarking on a journey of experiencing life's infinite ocean, but from within a boat that is already unbalanced. Then, due to our lop-sided starting place, we instinctively over-protect and excessively judge, which dramatically limits our possibility to experience life in its living fullness.

We often find ourselves needing to become more receptive if we are to have a fuller, more alive experience of reality. The more we become at ease in engaging with our neighbourhood, the more our ego's razor-gaze and left hemisphere's incessant grip can ease. The more these constraints ease, the more we experience life as it really is, unencumbered, raw and wild. It becomes easier to tune-in and resonate with everything around us; sensing and responding in a more open and honest way. With this attunement our creative potential flows more readily and we align with our true nature – our true Self. This requires a surrendering to experience unencumbered by abstract thought patterns of past or future. Our conscious awareness heightens to embrace all that is in the experience – we presence life. This is what phenomenology seeks to do in understanding the process of experiencing as an unfolding. Rather than perceiving something as an object or subject which is separate from us, it becomes a participatory experience. In this dynamic relationship between our self and the phenomenon an empathic envelopment of mutuality occurs. One can sense the other, not just through the initial sensory impulse as the event initially manifests, but through the depth of experience of relating with, across and through the event as it unfolds; an embrace that embodies the other. Our experience becomes much more than a sensory attention and response; it becomes a heartfelt communion that flows with love.

In our unattuned, dis-eased state it is a struggle to be able to engage in such a way without prejudices, preconceived judgements and anxieties creeping in. Yet as we experience more of reality beyond our own illusory confinements, there is hope in re-establishing a more wholesome way of attending to the world, one that is more balanced and yet never in balance (as that would predicate stasis rather than a process of becoming through continual attunement). We may then begin to ease up on our fear of the wild world. We might even start to love its wilful uncontrollable exuberance. The seeming chaos of life beyond the tidy yet artificial confines of abstract rationality may start to be experienced as intrinsically beautiful and wise beyond words.

As we allow for our receptivity to deepen with trust, we may begin to feel more engagement with all that we attend to. We may start to learn to love life through our unadulterated, direct experience of it. The realisation that we are co-creative participants in this enchanting synchronistic dance of life starts to dawn on us. As we open up to our true nature, our creative potential flows freer, allowing for an even greater intensity of beauty, wisdom and synchronicity to be revealed. This in turn heightens our responsiveness which is vital to any creative interaction; it is our authentic response to our engagement with life. We have to be wary of slipping back into an overly abstracted, isolated 'I' state that severs us from empathic relation and tunes out our creative flow. Like learning to ride a bike or swim, eventually, through practice, it becomes second nature, or rather we remember our primary nature once again. It is as if we have tuned into a radio station, happy to hear the tune clearly yet at once realising we are broadcasting live and playing within the music – we are literally 'on air'. We become musicians in the participatory dance of life.

There is no time like the present

We are here to awaken from the illusion of our separateness.

Thich Nhat Hanh[2]

As we have explored, definitive abstraction of 'content' from 'context' gives rise to dualistic false dichotomies, which generate an alienating sense of separation in our way of relating, engaging and attending in this world. Finding our attunement within ourselves and within our neighbourhood helps transcend this abstraction into participation. In learning to attune we open ourselves up to the flow of conscious love in all we participate in. As we learn to open up to love, we also recognise what obstructs the flow of love. Thoughts and feelings that dislocate us from the here-and-now extract us from the creative flow of life and, if left unchecked, can detract from our attuning dance of life. The reflective abstraction of our rational mind is a useful contribution to what makes us human as long as it is consciously allowed to loosen back into context – otherwise we risk imprisoning ourselves with our own self-reflexivity and so sever ourselves from synchronicity. It has been said that the diamond of truth has many facets and each torch light of our questing mind shines a beam on these multiple facets exposing aspects of the ultimate Truth from different perspectives. Yet if we get too attached to the torch beam, the mind may trap itself in its own projection seeing nothing but garish neon rather than the deeper shafts of illumination. In the words of the poet Rumi, 'So many garish lamps in the dying brain's lamp shop, Forget about them. Concentrate on essence, concentrate on Light.'[3]

As the psychological counsellor, spiritual teacher and writer Reshad Feild has said, if we are honest with ourselves we might see that much of what we do in life is motivated by barriers to love imposed by ourselves or others, which give rise to and are reinforced by quite natural and understandable feelings of resentment, envy and vanity.[4] Once aware of them, we can start to recognise that, while cultural conditioning clearly influences us, it is our internal condition, and our ability to open lovingly to where we actually are now, which sets up our attunement with life. Our ambition has to be to emanate love by breaking through these barriers in coming to terms with the feelings of resentment, envy and vanity they set in train. Let's take a look at each of these:

Resentment

To resist injustice with compassionate intent and honesty is courageous. But to hold resentment means to hold toxic feelings which sap away at us, undermining our ability to flow freely and fully as and where we are. Forgiveness and acceptance provide the antidote for resentment.

Envy

By accepting our self and others, we accept our experiences and relations for what they are, unencumbered by jealous envy. It is our accentuated sense of 'I' in comparative competition with 'other' that, if left unchecked, fuels jealous envy. As we rarefy our ego-boundaries by opening up through love, our envy dissipates.

Vanity

To feel a sense of achievement upon accomplishing something is a humble way of expressing love for ourselves and others involved. Yet when we gain a sense of superiority we create separation. We are each special in our own way, no one more special than the other regardless of their wisdom. As we consciously evolve we gain humility and compassion for others, not superiority over others.

To look at ourselves honestly and courageously helps dissolve barriers to love, as the barriers are consciously or unconsciously self-generated. In observing what motivates us, what lies behind our thoughts, feelings and behaviours we can gain insight into the sources of our barriers to love. The more conscious we become of our thoughts and feelings, the more we learn to recognise when we are holding back from the flow of love. In this way we take personal responsibility for how we attend to each moment.

And so we begin …

It is not a matter of whether we pray or weed the garden, whether we retire to a hermitage or drop into the local pub for a glass of beer and a chat. It is a matter of how and why we do these things; it is a question of attitude.

Cyprian Smith[5]

The more we learn to attune the more we encourage a way of attending through love. This is the beginning which is begun within every evolving moment. We are living, breathing bodymind portals through which Nature flows, and we are expressions of that Nature. As we reawaken the power of love within us we begin to heal the fragmentation of our psyche and so repair our estranged relation with ourselves, each other and Nature. This is the common ground of humankind's destiny within which we each have unique tunes to play. As the Pre-socratic philosopher Thales famously noted, all things are full of God. Every particle and every vibration within it flows with divinity and now is the time to consciously step into that river. Such is the utterly amazing beauty of life, and it comes with a humbling responsibility and reverence for Nature. Sufi scholar Henry Corbin wrote of this imaginal vision:

> We witness and participate in an entire ceremonial of meditation, a psalmody in two alternating voices, one human the other divine; and this psalmody perpetually reconstitutes, recreates … in each instant the act of primordial theophany is renewed in this psalmody of the Creator and the creature.[6]

Endnotes

Acknowledgments

1. Elliot, Thomas Stearns (1931) Preface to *Transit of Venus* (Poems by Harry Crosby).

Introduction

1. Bateson, Gregory (2000) *Steps to an Ecology of Mind, The University of Chicago Press*, Chicago, p.509.
2. Milne, Joseph (2010) *Henry George: The Ascent to the Good through Justice*, paper given to The Henry George Foundation, p.5.
3. Anderson, Ray & Robin White (2009) *Confessions of a Radical Industrialist*, Random House Business Books, New York, p.226.
4. Lagarde, Christine (2014) 'A New Multilateralism for the 21st Century', The Richard Dimbleby Lecture BBC 1, 4 February 2014.
5. Moore, C.J. (2014) http://kingabba.com/.

Chapter One

1. General reference for entire chapter: Curtis, Adam (2002) *The Century of the Self*, BBC4, London.
2. Forman, Jon (2010) 'The Economy of the Garden, Part Two', Huffington Post http://www.huffingtonpost.com/jon-foreman/the-economy-of-the-garden-part-two_b_700776.html.
3. Freud, Sigmund (1991) *The Future of An Illusion, In Civilization, Society and Religion*, Penguin, London, p.185.
4. Freud, Sigmund (1933) *New Introductory Lectures on Psychoanalysis*, W.W. Norton & Co., New York, p.106.
5. Gilbert, Jeremy (2014) *Common Ground: Democracy and Collectivity in an Age of Individualism*, Pluto Press, London, p.49–68.
6. Bernays, Edward (1928) *Propaganda*, cited by HRH The Prince of Wales *et al.* (2010) in *Harmony, A New Way of Looking At Our World*, Blue Door, London, p.175.
7. During, Alan Thein (1995) 'Are We Happy Yet?' *Ecopsychology*, ed. Theodore Roszak, *et al.* Kanner, San Francisco, Sierra Club, p.69.
8. Hamilton, Robert (1990) *Earthdream, The Marriage of Reason and Intuition*, Green Books, Hartland, p.146.
9. *Ibid.* p.173.
10. Crouch, Colin (2004) *Post-Democracy*, Polity, Malden, Massachusetts, p.19.
11. Gilbert, Jeremy (2014) p.33.

12. Kovel, Joel (1988) *The Radical Spirit: Essays on Psychoanalysis and Society,* Free Association, London, p.135.
13. Fisher, Andy (2013) *Radical Ecopsychology, Psychology in the Service of Life*, Suny Press, New York, p.87.
14. Omond, Tasmin (2014) 'Nothing Short of a Consumer Revolution Will Change the World', *Resurgence,* Issue 283, p.16–17.
15. Rawbotham, Michael (1998) *The Grip of Death, A Study of Modern Money, Debt Slavery and Destructive Economics*, Jon Carpenter, Charbury, p.53.
16. *Ibid.* p.320–323.

Chapter Two
1. Lewis, C.S. (1942) *The Screwtape Letters,* HarperCollins, New York, p.95.
2. Darwin, Charles (1859) *On the Origin of the Species by Means of Natural Selection: Or, the Preservation of Favoured Races in the Struggle for Life*, John Murray, London.
3. *Ibid.* p.155.
4. Dawkins, Richard (1989) *The Selfish Gene* (New ed.) Oxford University Press, Oxford, p.182.
5. Bateson, Gregory (2000) p.492.
6. *Ibid.* p.470–71.
7. *Ibid.* p.501.
8. Quinn, Daniel (1995) *Ishmael, An Adventure of the Mind and Spirit*, Bantam/ Turner, New York, p.127.
9. *Ibid.* p.133.
10. Shiva, Vandana (2014) 'Seed Freedom', *Resurgence,* Issue 278, p.10.
11. HRH The Prince of Wales *et al.* (2010) *Harmony, A New Way of Looking At Our World*, Blue Door, London, p.200.

Chapter Three
1. Maudsley, Henry (1867) cited in Radden, Jennifer (ed.) (2000) *The Nature of Melancholy, from Aristotle to Kristeva*, Oxford University Press, Oxford, p.27.
2. Gilbert, Jeremy (2014) p.13.
3. Berman, Morris (1981) *The Reenchantment of the World*, Cornell University Press, Ithaca, p.110.
4. Van Lysebeth, André (1995) *Tantra, The Cult of the Feminine*, Weiser Books, San Francisco, p.26.
5. Descartes, René, cited by André Van Lysebeth (1995) p.26.
6. Descartes, René cited by Morris Berman (1981) p.111.
7. Hobbes, Thomas (1949) *The Citizen*, Appleton Century Crofts, New York, p.13.
8. Einstein, Albert (1923) *Sidelights on Relativity: I. Ether and relativity. II. Geometry and experience* (translated by G.B. Jeffery, D.Sc., and W. Perrett, Ph.D). E.P. Dutton & Co., New York, p28.
9. McGilchrist, Iain (2009) *The Master and His Emissary, The Divided Brain and the Making of the Western World*, Yale University Press, New Haven, p.209.

Chapter Four

1. http://www.etymonline.com/index.php?search=philosophy&search-mode=none.
2. Soromenho-Marques, Viriato (2012) 'The Art of Living', *Resurgence,* Issue 272, p.41.
3. Kingsley, Peter (2003) *Reality,* The Golden Sufi Centre, Point Reyes, p387.
4. Cicero *(*1880–1885) *De Natura Deorum Libri Tres, Book I,* Cambridge Library Collection, cited http://en.wikipedia.org/wiki/Stoicism.
5. Abram, David (1997) *The Spell of the Sensuous,* Vantage Books, New York, p.97.
6. *Ibid.* p.98.
7. McGilchrist, Iain (2009) p.276.
8. Abram, David (1997) p.100.
9. Emerson, Ralph Waldo (2008) *Nature,* Penguin Books, London, p.31.
10. McGilchrist, Iain (2009) p.279.
11. Tarnas, Richard (2010) *The Passion of the Western Mind, Understanding the Ideas That Have Shaped Our World View,* Pimlico, London, p.68.
12. McGilchrist, Iain (2009) p.286.
13. http://plato.stanford.edu/entries/plotinus/.
14. http://en.wikipedia.org/wiki/Plotinus.
15. Hartshorne, Charles & William Reese (2000) *Philosophers Speak of God,* Humanity Books, New York, p.212.
16. Osbourne, Roger (2006) *Civilization, A New History of the Western World,* Jonathan Cape, London, Chapter Five.
17. Holland, Jack (2006) *Misogyny, The World's Oldest Prejudice,* Constable and Robinson Ltd, London, p.91.
18. Osbourne, Roger (2006) p.119.
19. Campbell, Joseph (1988) *The Power of Myth,* Doubleday, New York, p.197.
20. http://en.wikipedia.org/wiki/Eriugena.
21. Eriugena, John Scotus, Myra Uhlfelder, and Jean A. Potter, (1976) *Periphyseon: On the Division of Nature,* Book III, 678c. Bobbs-Merrill, Indianapolis, republished 2011 by Wipf & Stock Publishers, Oregon, p. 197.
22. Gnostic Gospel of Thomas, cited http://www.gospelofthomas.info/essays/stone.html.
23. Fincher, Susanne (2010) *Creating Mandalas, For Insight, Healing, and Self-Expression,* Shambhala, Boston, p.16.
24. Bonansea, Bernardino (1969) *Tommaso Campanella: Renaissance Pioneer of Modern Thought,* Catholic University of America Press, Washington, p.156.
25. Heidegger, Martin (1977) *Basic Writings: Martin Heidegger,* edited by David Farrell Krell, Routledge, London, p.275.
26. Strauss, Leo (1989) *An Introduction to Political Philosophy: Ten Essays, The Three Waves of Modernity,* Ed. Halail Gildin, Wayne State University Press, Detroit, p87–88.
27. Lear, Jonathan (2007) *Aristotle: The Desire to Understand,* Cambridge University Press, Cambridge, p.42.

28. Naydler, Jeremy (2009) *The Future of the Ancient World: Essays on the History of Consciousness*, Inner Traditions, Rochester, p.256.

Chapter Five

1. Baring, Anne & Jules Cashford (1993) *The Myth of the Goddess, Evolution of an Image*, Arkana Penguin Books, London, p.667.
2. Overy, Richard (2006) *The Times: Complete History of the World*, Times Books, London, p.36.
3. Buhner, Stephen Harrod (2004) *The Secret Teachings of Plants, The Intelligence of the Heart in the Direct Perception of Nature*, Bear & Company, Rochester, p.134.
4. Overy, Richard (2006) p.53.
5. Osbourne, Roger (2006) p.22.
6. http://www.animism.org.uk/.
7. Lawrence, David Herbert (1972) *The Complete Poems of D.H. Lawrence*, Vol. 1, Eds. Vivian De Sola Pinto and Warren Roberts, Heinemann, London, p.17.
8. Harner, Michael (1980) *The Way of The Shaman*, HarperCollins, New York.
9. Hutchins, Giles (2012) *The Nature of Business, Redesigning for Resilience*, Green Books, Totnes, p.66–67 extracted from a section co-created with Paul Francis.
10. Taylor, Steve (2005) *The Fall, The Insanity of the Ego in Human History and The Dawning of A New Era*, O Books, Winchester.
11. Hutchins, Giles (2012) p.65, from a section co-created with Denise DeLuca.
12. Harding, Stephan (2006) *Animate Earth, Science, Intuition and Gaia*, Green Books, Totnes, p.27.
13. Sheldrake, Rupert (1990) *The Rebirth of Nature, The Greening of Science and God*, Park Street Press, Rochester Vermont, p.18.
14. Taylor, Steve (2005) p.129.
15. Sheldrake, Rupert (1990) p.18.
16. *Ibid.*
17. Wilber, Ken (1981) *Up From Eden*, Quest Books, Wheaton.
18. Eisler, Riane (1988) *The Chalice & The Blade, Our History, Our Future*, Harper & Row, San Francisco.
19. Baring, Anne & Jules Cashford (1993) p.25.
20. Eisler, Riane (1988) p.45.
21. Eisler, Riane (1988) p.108.
22. Platon, Nicolas (1966) *Crete*, Nagel Publishers, Geneva, p.177.
23. Michell, John (1973) *The View Over Atlantis*, Abacus, London.
24. Harrison, Jane (1962) *Prolegomena to the study of Greek Religion*. Merlin Press, London, p.262.
25. Baring, Anne & Jules Cashford (1993) p.19.
26. Eisler, Riane (1988) p.75.
27. Gimbutas, Marija (1973) 'The Beginning of the Bronze Age in Europe and the Indo-Europeans: 3,000–2,500 BC', *Journal of Indo-European Studies 1*, p.202.

28. Baring, Anne (2013) *The Dream of the Cosmos, A Quest for the Soul*, Archive Publishing, http://www.annebaring.com/anbar20_bk_dreamwater_001.htm, Chapter Two.
29. Sheldrake, Rupert (1990) p.19.
30. Baring, Anne & Jules Cashford (1993) p.xi.
31. Baring, Anne & Jules Cashford (1993) p.661.

Chapter Six
1. Einstein, Albert cited in Hutchins, Giles (2012) p.20.
2. Barfield, Owen (1988) *Saving the Appearances, A Study in Idolatry*, Wesleyan University Press, Connecticut, p44.
3. *Ibid.* p.104.
4. *Ibid.* p.157.
5. *Ibid.* p.149.
6. *Ibid.* p.50.
7. *Ibid.* p.144.
8. McGilchrist, Iain (2009) p.27.
9. *Ibid.* p.133.
10. Wilson, Colin (1985) *A Criminal History of Mankind*, Grafton, London, p.144.
11. McGilchrist, Iain (2009) p.40.
12. *Ibid.* p.41.
13. *Ibid.* p.337.
14. *Ibid.* p.78.
15. *Ibid.* p.98.
16. *Ibid.* p.216.
17. *Ibid.* p.235.
18. *Ibid.* p.272.
19. *Ibid.* p.337.
20. *Ibid.* p.345.
21. *Ibid.* p.346.
22. Taylor, Steve (2005) p.157.

Chapter Seven
1. Shakespeare, William (1606) *King Lear, Act 1 Scene 2* http://www.shakespeare-monologues.org/plays/32?expand=1.
2. Braungart, Michael & William McDonough (2009) *Cradle to Cradle, Re-making the Way we Make Things*, Vintage, London, p.120.
3. Margulis, Lynn & Dorion Sagan (2001) 'Marvellous microbes', *Resurgence* Issue 206, p.10–12.
4. Lipton, Bruce (2001) *Insight into Cellular Consciousness, Reprinted from Bridges, 2001 Vol 12(1):5 ISEEM*, cited in https://www.brucelipton.com/resource/article/insight-cellular-consciousness.
5. Wordsworth, William (1815) Essay Supplementary to Preface, cited in Rayner, Alan (2011) *NatureScope*, O Books, Winchester, p.68.
6. Buhner, Stephen Harrod (2004) *The Secret Teachings of Plants, The Intelligence*

of the Heart in the Direct Perception of Nature, Bear & Company, Rochester, p.42.

7. de Quincey, Christian (2002) *Radical Nature, The Soul of Matter*, Park Street Press, Rochester, p.77.

8. Buhner, Stephen Harrod (2004) p.63.

9. *Ibid.* p.53.

10. de Quincey, Christian (2002) p.210.

11. Harding, Stephan (2006) *Animate Earth, Science, Intuition and Gaia*, Green Books, Totnes, p.163.

12. *Ibid.* p.166.

13. *Ibid.* p.167.

14. *Ibid.* p.169.

15. Stamets, Paul (2005) *Mycelium Running, How Mushrooms Can Help Save the World*, Ten Speed Press, Berkeley, p.2.

16. Laszlo, Ervin (1999) *The Whispering Pond*, Element Books, Shaftesbury, p.113.

17. Jung, Carl (1973) *The Collected Works of C.G.Jung,* (ed. Gerhard Adler *et al.*) Routledge, London, para. 610.

18. http://www.animalspirit.org/.

19. Watson, Lyall (1974) *SuperNature, A natural history of the supernatural*, Coronet, Aylesbury, p.247.

20. De La Warr, George (1969) *Do Plants Feel Emotion*, Electro Technology cited in Watson, Lyall (1974).

21. Watson, Lyall (1986) *Earthworks, Ideas on the edge of natural history*. Hodder and Stoughton, Sevenoaks, p.47.

22. Grof, Stanislav & Hal Bennett (1993) *The Holotropic Mind, Three levels of Human Consciousness and How They Shape Our Lives,* HarperCollins, New York, p.18.

23. Jung, Carl (1976) *Letters 2 1951–1961*, (ed. Gerhard Adler), Princeton University Press, Princeton, Letter to Miguel Serrano, 1960 in *Letters 2*, p. 595.

Chapter Eight

1. *Book of Genesis* 1:3.

2. Haisch, Bernard (2006) *The God Theory, Universes, Zero-point Fields, and What's Behind it All*, Weiser, San Francisco, p.93.

3. *Ibid.* p.117.

4. *Ibid.* p.115.

5. Kaku, Michio (2005) *Unifying The Universe*, New Scientist, Issue 16, p. 48.

6. Samanta-Laughton, Manjir (2006) *Punk Science, Inside The Mind of God*, O Books, Winchester, p.138.

7. Swimme, Brian (1999) *The Hidden Heart of The Cosmos, Humanity and the New Story*, Orbis Books, New York, p.98–102.

8. Laszlo, Ervin (1999) p.214.

9. Samanta-Laughton, Manjir (2006) p.195–200.

10. *Ibid.* p.210.

11. Knight, Dolly & Jonathan Stromberg (2005) *Rethinking the Basis of Technology*, Centre of Implosion Research, Plymouth.

Chapter Nine

1. Avens, Roberts (1984) *New Gnosis, Heidegger, Hillman, and Angels*, Spring Publications, Zurich, p.109.
2. Bergson, Henri (1946) *The Creative Mind*, Citadel Press, New Jersey, p.34.
3. James, William (1996) *A Pluralistic Universe*, University of Nebraska Press, Nebraska, p.212.
4. James, William (1929) *The Varieties of Religious Experience*, Longmans, Green and Co, London, New York, p. 388.
5. http://en.wikipedia.org/wiki/William_James.
6. de Quincey, Christian (2002) p.249–250.
7. Griffin, David Ray (2001) *Reenchantment without Supernaturalism, A Process Philosophy of Religion*, Cornell University Press, Ithaca, p.130–131.
8. Christ, Carol P (2003) *She Who Changes, Re-imagining the Divine in the World*, Palgrave Macmillian, New York, p.62.
9. McGilchrist, Iain (2009) p.151.
10. Keller, Catherine (2008) *On the Mystery, Discerning Divinity In Process*, Fortress Press, Minneapolis, p.xiv.
11. Kumar, Satish (2002) *You Are Therefore I Am, A Declaration of Dependence*, Green Books, Totnes, p.30.
12. Keller, Catherine (2008) p.xii.
13. *Ibid.* p.42.
14. King, Ursula (1996) *Spirit Fire, The Life and Vision of Teilhard de Chardin*, Orbis Books, New York.
15. Van Lysebeth, André (1995) *Tantra, The Cult of the Feminine*, Weiser Books, San Francisco, p.16.
16. Skrbina, David (2007) *Panpsychism in the West*, MIT Press, Cambridge MA, p.169.
17. http://en.wikipedia.org/wiki/Pierre_Teilhard_de_Chardin.
18. Bohm, David (1957) *Causality and Chance in Modern Physics*, Routledge, London, p.163.
19. Skrbina, David (2007) p.205.
20. http://www.thomasberry.org/Essays/DemocracyCosmologyAndTheGreat Work Of ThomasBerry.html.
21. Kumar, Satish (2002) p.181.
22. Skrbina, David (2007) p.269.
23. de Quincey, Christian (2002) p.161.
24. *Ibid.* p.263.
25. http://www.greatchange.org/ov-aurobindo,life_divine.html.

Chapter Ten

1. Goethe, Johann (1988) *Sautliche Werke*, ed. K. Richter, 21 Vols, Carl Hanser Verlag, Munich, p.272.

 2. Bortoft, Henri (1996) *The Wholeness of Nature*, Lindisfarne Books, New York, p.74.
 3. McGilchrist, Iain (2009) p.199.
 4. Merleau-Ponty, Maurice (1945) *Phenomenology of Perception*, Routledge, London.
 5. Abram, David (1997) p.66.
 6. *Ibid.* p.68.
 7. *Ibid.* p.206.
 8. Watts, Michael (2011) *The Philosophy of Heidegger*, Acumen, Durham, p.66.
 9. Bortoft, Henri (2012) *Taking Appearance Seriously, The Dynamic Way of Seeing in Goethe and European Thought*, Floris Books, Edinburgh, p.17.
10. Bortoft, Henri (1996) p.71.
11. Sardello, Robert (2006) *Silence, The Mystery of Wholeness,* North Atlantic Books, Berkeley, p.82.
12. Confucius cited in Hutchins, Giles (2012) p.31.
13. Parsons, Tony (1995) *The Open Secret,* Open Secret Publishing, p.23.
14. *Ibid.* p.46.
15. Fisher, Andy (2013) pxiii.
16. *Ibid.* p.7.
17. Abram, David (1997) p.257.
18. Totton, Nick (2011) *Wild Therapy, Undomesticating Inner and Outer Worlds*, PCCS Books, Ross-on-Wye, p.19.

Chapter Eleven
 1. Marley, Bob (1980) *Redemption Song, Uprising*, Bob Marley and the Wailers.
 2. Stevens, Anthony (1994) *Jung, A Very Short Introduction*, Oxford University Press, Oxford, p.81.
 3. *Ibid.* p.24.
 4. *Ibid.* p.129.
 5. *Ibid.* p.84.
 6. Key, David & Margaret Kerr (2013) *Transpersonal Patterns in the Natural Change Project*, Journal of Transpersonal Psychology.
 7. Gendlin, Eugene (1981) *Focusing*, Bantam, New York, p.76.
 8. Choy, Peter Chin Kean (1998) *T'ai Chi Chi Kung, Fifteen Ways to a Happier You*, Kyle Cathie Ltd, London, p.80–81.
 9. Sumedho, Ajahn (2004) *Intuitive Awareness*, Amaravati Publications, Herts, p.88.
10. Layard, Richard (2011) 'A Better Way of Life', *Resurgence*, Issue 269, p.16.
11. Maxwell, Rashid (2012) 'Lessons from the Bees', *Resurgence*, Issue 272, p.38.
12. Smith, Cyprian (2004) *The Way of Paradox, Spiritual Life As Taught By Meister Eckhart*, Darton Longman and Todd, London, p.13.
13. Naydler, Jeremy (2009) *The Future of the Ancient World, Essays on the History of Consciousness,* Inner Traditions, Rochester, p.90–91.
14. Baring, Anne & Jules Cashford (1993) p.676.
15. Coleridge, Samuel Taylor (1817) *Biographia Literaria*, Princeton University Press, Princeton, p. 167.
16. Corbin, Henry (1969) *Alone with the Alone, Creative Imagination in the Sufism of Ibn'Arabi*, Princeton University Press, Bollingen Series XCI, Princeton, p.179.

17. Stevens, Anthony (1994) p.154.
18. Dillard, Annie (1982) *Teaching a Stone to Talk*, HarperCollins, New York, p.91–92.
19. Blake, William (1961) *Complete Poetry and Prose*, ed. Geoffrey Keynes, Nonesuch Press, London, p.835.

Chapter Twelve
1. De Saint-Exupéry, Antoine (2002) *The Little Prince*, Egmont, London, p.68.
2. http://heartmastery.com/about-us/heart-facts.
3. Buhner, Stephen Harrod (2004) p.83.
4. *Ibid.* p.86.
5. *Ibid.* p.101.
6. *Ibid.* p.102.
7. Pert, Candace (1998) *Molecules of Emotion*, Simon and Schuster Ltd., London.
8. May, Gerald (1991) *The Awakened Heart, Opening Yourself to the Love You Need*, Harper Collins, New York, p.195.
9. *Ibid.* p.191.
10. Romanyshyn, Robert (2002) *Ways of the Heart, Essays Towards an Imaginal Psychology*, Trivium Publications, Pittsburgh, p.159.
11. Heraclitus, cited in Baring, Anne (2013) *The Dream of the Cosmos, A Quest for the Soul*, Archive Publishing, Chapter 11 http://www.annebaring.com/anbar20_ bk_dreamwater2.htm.
12. Romanyshyn, Robert (2002) p.44.
13. Bachelard, Gaston (1971*) The Poetics of Reverie*, Beacon Press, Boston, Chapter 2, Section 3.
14. Romanyshyn, Robert (2002), p.38.
15. *Ibid.* p.38.
16. Sardello, Robert (2006) *Silence, The Mystery of Wholeness*, North Atlantic Books, Berkeley, p.13.
17. *Ibid.* p.13.
18. *Ibid.* p.3.
19. *Ibid.* p.8.
20. Debussey, Claude cited in Koomey, Jonathan (2001) *Turning Numbers into Knowledge, Mastering the Art of Problem Solving*, Analytics Press, Burlingame, p.96.

Chapter Thirteen
1. Luther Standing Bear, Chief of the Oglala http://www.indigenouspeople.net/standbea.htm.
2. Lushwala, Arkan (2012) *The Time of the Black Jaguar, An Offering of Indigenous Wisdom for the Continuity of Life on Earth*, Arkan Lushwala, Ribera, p.153.
3. Small, Meredith (1999) *Our Babies, Ourselves, How Biology and Culture Shape the Way We Parent*, Anchor Books, New York.
4. Illardi, Stephan (2009) *The Depression Cure*, DeCapo Press, Cambridge, Massachusetts.

5. Diamond, Stanley (1974) *In Search of the Primitive, A Critique of Civilization*, Transaction, New Brunswick.
6. McGilchrist, Iain (2009) p.461.
7. Martin, Calvin Luther (1999) *The Way of the Human Being*, Yale University Press, New Haven, p.62.
8. *Ibid.* p.79.
9. Fisher, Andy (2013) p.96.
10. Shepard, Paul (1996) *The Others, How Animals Made Us Human*, Island, Washington, p.5.
11. Fisher, Andy (2013) p.96.
12. Lushwala, Arkan (2012) p.19.
13. *Ibid.* p.21.
14. *Ibid.* p.80.
15. Zimmerman, Mary Jane (2004) *Being Nature's Mind: Indigenous Ways of Knowing and Planetary Consciousness,* p.20, http://www.delvingdeeper.org/pdfs/being.pdf.
16. Thoreau, Henry David (1862) *Walking Part II*, cited http://thoreau.eserver.org/walking2.html.
17. Macfarlane, Robert (2007) *The Wild Places*, Granta Books, London, p.31.
18. Griffiths, Jay (2006) *Wild, An Elemental Journey*, Penguin Books, London, p.102.
19. Totton, Nick (2011) p.58.
20. *Ibid.* p.41–42.
21. *Ibid.* p.91.
22. Keller, Catherine (2008) p.45.

Chapter Fourteen
1. Jung, Carl (1990) *The Undiscovered Self, in Collected Works of Carl Gustav Jung*, Vol. 10, Princeton University Press, Princeton, p.59–60.
2. Lushwala, Arkan (2012) p.82.
3. Russell, Bertrand http://www.goodreads.com/author/show/17854.Bertrand_Russell.
4. Kuhn, Thomas (1996) *The Structure of Scientific Revolutions*, University of Chicago Press, Chicago.
5. Speth, James Gustave (2008) *The Bridge at the Edge of the World, Capitalism, the Environment, and Crossing from Crisis to Sustainability*, Yale University Press, New Haven, p.204.
6. *Ibid.* p207.
7. *Ibid.* p235.
8. Van Lysebeth, André (1995) p.67.
9. Sheldrake, Rupert (1990) p.189.
10. Macartney, Tim (2007) *Finding Earth Finding Soul, The Invisible Path to Authentic Leadership*, Mona Press, Embercombe, p.180.
11. http://www.ottoscharmer.com/.
12. Coleman, Eliot (2014) 'The Importance of Soil', *Resurgence*, Issue 283, p.10.
13. Confino, Jo (2014*),* 'How to lead with integrity', interview with Paul Polman, *The Guardian*, Guardian Sustainable Business Awards, 15th May.

14. Holdrege, Craig (2014) 'Rooted In The World', *Resurgence*, Issue 282, p.43–45.
15. Senge, Peter *et al.* (2004) *Presence, Human Purpose and the Field of the Future*, SoL, Cambridge, Massachusetts, p.187.
16. Dillard, Anne cited in http://www.couragerenewal.org/parker/writings/leading-from-within.

Chapter Fifteen
1. Mitchell, Stephen (1999) *Tao Te Ching, Lao Tzu, An Illustrated Journey* (translated), Frances Lincoln, London, section 42.
2. Doczi, György (1981) *The Power of Limits*, Shambhala Publications, Boston, p.2.
3. Hutchins, Giles (2012) p.52.
4. Field, Reshad (1990) *The Alchemy of the Heart*, Element, Shaftesbury, p.53.
5. Doczi, György (1981) p.5.
6. Maira, Shakti (2014) 'To Fit Together', *Resurgence*, Issue 282, p.47.
7. Lovins, Hunter (2011) Speech at Tomorrow's Natural Business event, London, 11 November.
8. Hutchins, Giles (2012) p.52.
9. Van Lysebeth, André (1995) p.164.
10. *Ibid.* p.119.
11. *Ibid.* p.9.
12. *Ibid.* p.109.
13. Abram, David (1997) p.27.
14. Lushwala, Arkan (2012) p.129.
15. Lushwala, Arkan (2012) p.121.
16. Bourgeault, Cynthia (2010) *The Meaning of Mary Magdalene*, Shambhala, Boston, p.61.

Chapter Sixteen
1. O'Donohue, John (1997) p.274.
2. Buhner, Stephen Harrod (2004) p.18.
3. Abram, David (1997) p.216.
4. Rayner, Alan (2011) *NaturesScope*, O Books, Winchester, p.166.
5. *Ibid.* p.67.
6. McGilchrist, Iain (2009) p.71.
7. Rayner, Alan (2013) *Inclusional Sustainability, A Natural Way of Life*, p.6, http://www.bestthinking.com/articles/science/biology_and_nature/ecology/inclusional-sustainability?tab=article.
8. Rayner, Alan (2013) *The Fluid Boundary Logic of Fungi*, Common Knowledge 19:2 Duke University Press, Durham NC, p. 267.
9. Rayner, Alan (2011) p.118.
10. *Ibid.* p.133.

Chapter Seventeen
1. Drucker, Peter cited http://thenatureofbusiness.org/2012/10/04/leading-with-love/.

2. Bateson, Gregory (2000) p.507.
3. Schumacher, E.F (1973) *Small is Beautiful, A Study of Economics as if People Mattered*, Penguin Group, London, p.64.
4. *Ibid.* p.77.
5. Coomaraswamy, Ananda (1936) *The Love of Art*, broadcasted in Educational Programmes, WIXAL, Boston, cited in Temenos Number 13 (1992) The Temenos Academy, Ashford, p.55.
6. Sennett, Richard (2008) *The Craftsman*, Penguin Books, London.
7. Crawford, Matthew (2009) *The Case For Working With Your Hands*, Penguin Books, London.
8. Kojeve, Alexandre (1989) *Introduction to the Reading of Hegel: Lectures on the Phenomenology of Spirit*, Cornell University Press, Ithaca, p.27.
9. Crawford, Matthew (2009) p.21.
10. Eisenstein, Charles (2011) *Sacred Economics, Money, Gift & Society in the Age of Transition*, Evolver Editions, Berkeley, p.414.
11. Coomaraswamy, Ananda (1936) cited in Temenos Number 13 (1992) p.59.
12. Nesfield-Cookson, Bernard (1994) *Rudolf Steiner's Vision of Love*, Sophia Books, London, p.19.
13. *Ibid.* p.29.
14. Mother Teresa, cited in Hutchins, Giles (2012) p.6.
15. http://www.heartmath.org/.
16. Kline, Nancy (1999) *Time to Think, Listening to Ignite the Human Mind*, Cassell Illustrated, London, p.196.
17. Moore, Alan (2011) *No Straight Lines, Making Sense of our Non-linear World*, Bloodstone Books, Cambridge. p.181–182.
18. Scharmer, Otto & Katrin Kaufer (2013) *Leading From The Emerging Future, From Ego-System To Eco-System Economies*, Berret-Koehler Publishers, San Francisco, p.244.
19. Eisenstein, Charles (2011) p.187.
20. http://www.ancienthealingways.co.uk/.
21. Gilbert, Jeremy (2014) p.27.
22. *Ibid.* p.35.
23. Hutchins, Giles (2012) *The Nature of Business, Redesigning for Resilience*, Green Books, Totnes.
24. Mang, Pamela & Bill Reed (2012) *Designing from Place, a Regenerative Framework and Methodology*, Building Research & Information, 40:1, p.23–38.
25. *Ibid.* p.34.
26. *Ibid.* p.26.
27. Bortoft, Henri (2012) *Taking Appearance Seriously, The Dynamic Way of Seeing in Goethe and European Thought*, Floris Books, Edinburgh, p.58.
28. Robinson, Simon & Maria Moraes Robinson (2014) *Holonomics: Business Where People and Planet Matter*, Floris Books, Edinburgh, p.14–15.
29. Reynolds, Fiona (2014) 'Seeing Nature', *Resurgence*, Issue 284, p.63.
30. Williams, Rowan (2014) 'What the Body Knows', *Resurgence*, Issue 283, p.35.
31. Blake, William (1961) *Complete Poetry and Prose*, ed. Geoffrey Keynes, Nonesuch Press, London.

Chapter Eighteen
1. K. Khosa cited in Malik, Keshav (1992) 'Conversations with a Painter', *Temenos* Number 13, Temenos Academy, Ashford, p100.
2. Thich Nhat Hanh cited in http://www.goodreads.com/quotes/5258-we-are-here-to-awaken-from-our-illusion-of-separateness.
3. Rumi cited in http://rumifestival.org/wordpress/?page_id=745.
4. Feild, Reshad (1990) *The Alchemy of the Heart*, Element, Shaftesbury, p30–35.
5. Smith, Cyprian (2004) p.94.
6. Corbin, Henry (1969) p.249.

References

Abram, David (1997) *The Spell of the Sensuous*, Vantage Books, New York.

Anderson, Ray & Robin White (2009) *Confessions of a Radical Industrialist*, Random House Business Books, New York.

Avens, Roberts (1984) *New Gnosis, Heidegger, Hillman, and Angels*, Spring Publications, Zurich.

Barfield, Owen (1988) *Saving the Appearances, A Study in Idolatry*, Wesleyan University Press, Connecticut.

Baring, Anne & Jules Cashford (1993) *The Myth of the Goddess, Evolution of an Image*, Arkana Penguin Books, London.

Baring, Anne (2013) *The Dream of the Cosmos, A Quest for the Soul*, Archive Publishing, http://www.annebaring.com/anbar20_bk_dreamwater_001.htm

Bateson, Gregory (2000) *Steps to an Ecology of Mind*, The University of Chicago Press, Chicago.

Berman, Morris (1981) *The Reenchantment of the World*, Cornell University Press, Ithaca.

Blake, William (1961) *Complete Poetry and Prose*, edited by Geoffrey Keynes, Nonesuch Press, London.

Bachelard, Gaston (1971) *The Poetics of Reverie*, Beacon Press, Boston.

Bergson, Henri (1946) *The Creative Mind*, Citadel Press, New Jersey.

Bohm, David (1957) *Causality and Chance in Modern Physics*, Routledge, London.

Bonansea, Bernardino (1969) *Tommaso Campanella: Renaissance Pioneer of Modern Thought*, Catholic University of America Press, Washington.

Bortoft, Henri (1996) *The Wholeness of Nature*, Lindisfarne Books, New York.

—, (2012) *Taking Appearance Seriously, The Dynamic Way of Seeing in Goethe and European Thought*, Floris Books, Edinburgh.

Bourgeault, Cynthia (2010) *The Meaning of Mary Magdalene*, Shambhala, Boston.

Braungart, Michael & William McDonough (2009) *Cradle to Cradle, Re-making the Way We Make Things*, Vintage, London.

Buhner, Stephen Harrod (2004) *The Secret Teachings of Plants, The Intelligence of the Heart in the Direct Perception of Nature*, Bear & Company, Rochester.

Campbell, Joseph (1988) *The Power of Myth*, Doubleday, New York.

Capra, Fritjof (2003) *The Hidden Connections: A Science for Sustainable Living*, Flamingo, London.

Choy, Peter Chin Kean (1998) *T'ai Chi Chi Kung, Fifteen Ways to a Happier Yo*u, Kyle Cathie Ltd, London.

Christ, Carol P (2003) *She Who Changes, Re-imagining the Divine in the World*, Palgrave Macmillian, New York.

Cicero *(1880–1885) De Natura Deorum Libri Tres, Book I,* Cambridge Library Collection, Cambridge.

Coleman, Eliot (2014) 'The Importance of Soil', *Resurgence,* Issue 283.

Coleridge, Samuel Taylor (1817) *Biographia Literaria,* Princeton University Press, Princeton.

Confino, Jo (2014*)* 'How to lead with integrity', interview with Paul Polman, *The Guardian,* The Guardian Sustainable Business Awards, May 15, 2014.

Coomaraswamy, Ananda (1936) *The Love of Art,* broadcasted in Educational Programmes, WIXAL, Boston, cited in Temenos Number 13 (1992) The Temenos Academy, Ashford.

Corbin, Henry (1969) *Alone with the Alone, Creative Imagination in the Sufism of Ibn'Arabi,* Princeton University Press, Bollingen Series XCI, Princeton.

Corry, Stephen (2011) *Tribal Peoples, for Tomorrow's World,* Freeman Press, Alcester.

Crawford, Matthew (2009) *The Case For Working With Your Hands,* Penguin Books, London.

Crouch, Colin (2004) *Post-Democracy,* Polity, Malden, Massachusetts.

Curtis, Adam (2002) *The Century of the Self,* BBC4, London.

Darwin, Charles (1859) *On the Origin of the Species by Means of Natural Selection: Or, the Preservation of Favoured Races in the Struggle for Life,* J. Murray, London.

Dawkins, Richard (1989) *The Selfish Gene,* Oxford University Press, Oxford.

—, (1999) *Unweaving The Rainbow,* Penguin Books, London.

De Botton, Alain (2009) *The Pleasures and Sorrows of Work,* Penguin Books, London.

De Botton, Alain (2004) *Status Anxiety,* Hamish Hamilton, London.

De Chardin *(see* Teilhard de Chardin).

De Saint-Exupéry, Antoine (2002) *The Little Prince,* Egmont, London.

de Quincey, Christian (2002) *Radical Nature, The Soul of Matter,* Park Street Press, Rochester.

Diamond, Stanley (1974) *In Search of the Primitive, A Critique of Civilisation,* Transaction, New Brunswick.

Dillard, Annie (1982) *Teaching a Stone to Talk,* HarperCollins, New York.

Doczi, György (1981) *The Power of Limits,* Shambhala Publications, Boston.

During, Alan Thein (1995) 'Are We Happy Yet?' *Ecopsychology,* ed Theodore Roszak, *et al.* Sierra Club, San Francisco.

Einstein, Albert (1923) *Sidelights on Relativity: I. Ether and relativity. II. Geometry and experience* (tran. G.B. Jeffery and W. Perrett) E.P. Dutton & Co., New York.

Eisenstein, Charles (2011) *Sacred Economics, Money, Gift & Society in the Age of Transition,* Evolver Editions, Berkeley.

Eisler, Riane (1988) *The Chalice & The Blade, Our History, Our Future,* Harper & Row, San Francisco.

Emerson, Ralph Waldo (2008) *Nature,* Penguin Books, London.

Eriugena, John Scotus, Myra Uhlfelder, & Jean A. Potter (1976) *Periphyseon: On the Division of Nature,* Book III, Wipf & Stock Publishers, Oregon.

Field, Reshad (1990) *The Alchemy of the Heart*, Element, Shaftesbury.

Fincher, Susanne (2010) *Creating Mandalas, For Insight, Healing, and Self-Expression*, Shambhala, Boston.

Fisher, Andy (2013) *Radical Ecopsychology, Psychology in the Service of Life*, Suny Press, New York.

Forman, Jon (2010) 'The Economy of the Garden' – Part Two, Huffington Post http://www.huffingtonpost.com/jon-foreman/the-economy-of-the-garden-part-two_b_700776.html

Freud, Sigmund (1933) *New Introductory Lectures on Psychoanalysis,* W.W.Norton, New York.

— (1991) 'The Future of An Illusion', in *Civilization, Society and Religion*, Penguin, London.

Gendlin, Eugene (1981) *Focusing*, Bantam, New York.

Gilbert, Jeremy (2014) *Common Ground: Democracy and Collectivity in an Age of Individualism*, Pluto Press, London.

Gimbutas, Marija (1973) *The Beginning of the Bronze Age in Europe and the Indo-Europeans: 3,000–2,500 BC*, Journal of Indo-European Studies 1.

Gnostic Gospel of Thomas, cited http://www.gospelofthomas.info/essays/stone.html

Goethe, Johann von (1988) *Sautliche Werke*, ed. K. Richter, 21 Vols, Carl Hanser Verlag, Munich.

Grof, Stanislav & Hal Bennett (1993) *The Holotropic Mind, Three levels of Human Consciousness and How They Shape Our Lives*, HarperCollins, New York.

Griffin, David Ray (2001) *Reenchantment without Supernaturalism, A Process Philosophy of Religion*, Cornell University Press, Ithaca.

Griffiths, Jay (1999) *Pip Pip, A Sideways Look At Time*, Flamingo, London.

— (2006) *Wild, An Elemental Journey*, Penguin Books, London.

Haisch, Bernard (2006) *The God Theory, Universes, Zero-point Fields, and What's Behind it All*, Weiser, San Francisco.

Hamilton, Robert (1990) *Earthdream, The Marriage of Reason and Intuition*, Green Books, Hartland.

Harding, Stephan (2006) *Animate Earth, Science, Intuition and Gaia*, Green Books, Totnes.

Harner, Michael (1990) *The Way of the Shaman*, HarperCollins, New York.

Harrison, Jane (1962) *Prolegomena to the study of Greek Religion*, Merlin Press, London.

Hart, William (1988) *The Art of Living, Vipassana Meditation as taught by S. N.Goenka*, Vipassana Research Institute, Igatpuri.

Hartshorne, Charles & William Reese (2000) *Philosophers Speak of God*, Humanity Books, New York.

Heidegger, Martin (1977) *Basic Writings: Martin Heidegger*, ed. David Farrell Krell, Routledge, London.

Hobbes, Thomas (1949) *The Citizen*, Appleton Century Crofts, New York.

Holland, Jack (2006) *Misogyny, The World's Oldest Prejudice*, Constable and Robinson, London.

Holdrege, Craig (2014) 'Rooted In The World', *Resurgence*, Issue 282.

HRH The Prince of Wales *et al.* (2010) *Harmony, A New Way of Looking At Our World*, Blue Door, London.

Hutchins, Giles (2012) *The Nature of Business, Redesigning for Resilience*, Green Books, Totnes.

Illardi, Stephan (2009) *The Depression Cure*, DeCapo Press, Cambridge, Massachusetts.

James, William (1929) *The Varieties of Religious Experience*, Longmans, Green and Co, London, New York.

— (1996) *A Pluralistic Universe*, University of Nebraska Press, Nebraska.

Jung, Carl (1973) *The Collected Works of C.G. Jung*, ed. Gerhard Adler *et al.* Routledge, London.,

— (1976) *Letters 2*, 1951–1961, ed. Gerhard Adler, Princeton University Press, Princeton.

— (1990) *The Undiscovered Self*, in *Collected Works of Carl Gustav Jung*, vol. 10, Princeton University Press, Princeton.

Kaku, Michio (2005) 'Unifying The Universe', *New Scientist*, Issue 16, April 2005.

Keller, Catherine (2008) *On the Mystery, Discerning Divinity In Process*, Fortress Press, Minneapolis.

Key, David & Margaret Kerr (2013) 'Transpersonal Patterns in the Natural Change Project', *Journal of Transpersonal Psychology*.

King, Ursula (1996) *Spirit Fire, The Life and Vision of Teilhard de Chardin*, Orbis Books, New York.

Kingsley, Peter (2003) *Reality*, The Golden Sufi Centre, Point Reyes.

Kline, Nancy (1999) *Time to Think, Listening to Ignite the Human Mind*, Cassell Illustrated, London.

Knight, Dolly & Stromberg Jonathan (2005) *Rethinking the Basis of Technology*, Centre of Implosion Research, Plymouth.

Kojeve, Alexandre (1989) *Introduction to the Reading of Hegel: Lectures on the Phenomenology of Spirit*, Cornell University Press, Ithaca.

Koomey, Jonathan (2001) *Turning Numbers into Knowledge, Mastering the Art of Problem Solving*, Analytics Press, Burlingame.

Kovel, Joel (1988) *The Radical Spirit: Essays on Psychoanalysis and Society*, Free Association London.

— (2007) *The Enemy of Nature, The End of Capitalism or the End of the World?* Zed Books, London.

Kuhn, Thomas (1996) *The Structure of Scientific Revolutions*, University of Chicago Press, Chicago.

Kumar, Satish (1992) *No Destination, An Autobiography*, Green Books, Totnes.

— (2002) *You Are Therefore I Am, A Declaration of Dependence*, Green Books, Totnes.

Lagarde, Christine (2014) 'A New Multilateralism for the 21st Century', The Richard Dimbleby Lecture, BBC 1, 4 February 2014.

Laszlo, Ervin (1999) *The Whispering Pond*, Element Books, Shaftesbury.

Lancaster, Brian (2006) *The Essence of Kabbalah*, Eagle Editions, Royston.

Lawrence, David Herbert (1972) *The Complete Poems of D.H. Lawrence*, Eds. Vivian De Sola Pinto and Warren Roberts, Heinemann, London.

Layard, Richard (2011) 'A Better Way of Life', *Resurgence*, Issue 269.

Lear, Jonathan (2007) *Aristotle: The Desire to Understand*, Cambridge University Press, Cambridge.

Lewis, C.S. (1942) *The Screwtape Letters*, HarperCollins Publishers, New York.

Lipton, Bruce & Steve Bhaerman (2009) *Spontaneous Evolution, Our Positive Future*, Hay House, New York.

Lipton, Bruce (2001) *Insight into Cellular Consciousness*, Reprinted from *Bridges, 2001 Vol 12(1):5 ISEEM* Cited https://www.brucelipton.com/resource/article/insight-cellular-consciousness.

Lushwala, Arkan (2012) *The Time of the Black Jaguar, An Offering of Indigenous Wisdom for the Continuity of Life on Earth*, Lushwala, Ribera.

Macartney, Tim (2007) *Finding Earth Finding Soul, The Invisible Path to Authentic Leadership*, Mona Press, Embercombe.

Macfarlane, Robert (2007) *The Wild Places*, Granta Books, London.

Macy, Joanna & Chris Johnstone (2012) *Active Hope, How to Face the Mess We're in Without Going Crazy*, New World Library, Novato.

Maira, Shakti (2014) 'To Fit Together', *Resurgence*, Issue 282.

Malik, Keshav (1992) 'Conversations with a Painter', *Temenos* Number 13, Temenos Academy, Ashford.

Mang, Pamela & Bill Reed (2012) *Designing From Place, a Regenerative Framework and Methodology*, Building Research & Information, 40:1, p.23–38.

Margulis, Lynn & Dorion Sagan (2001) 'Marvellous microbes', *Resurgence,* Issue 206.

Martin, Calvin Luther (1999) *The Way of the Human Being*, Yale University Press, New Haven.

Maudsley, Henry (1867) cited in Radden, Jennifer (ed.) (2000) *The Nature of Melancholy, from Aristotle to Kristeva*, Oxford University Press, Oxford.

May, Gerald (1991) *The Awakened Heart, Opening Yourself To The Love You Need*, Harper Collins, New York.

Maxwell, Rashid (2012) 'Lessons from the Bees', *Resurgence*, Issue 272.

McGilchrist, Iain (2009) *The Master and His Emissary, The Divided Brain and the Making of the Western World*, Yale University Press, New Haven.

Merleau-Ponty, Maurice (1945) *Phenomenology of Perception*, Routledge, London.

Michell, John (1973) *The View Over Atlantis*, Abacus, London.

Milne, Joseph (2008) 'Metaphysics and the Cosmic Order', *Temenos Academy Papers,* The Temenos Academy, Ashford.

— (2010) 'Henry George: The Ascent to the Good through Justice', paper given to The Henry George Foundation, London.

— (2013) 'The Mystical Cosmos', *Temenos Academy Papers,* The Temenos Academy, Ashford.

Mitchell, Stephen (1999) *Tao Te Ching, Lao Tzu, An Illustrated Journey* (translated), Frances Lincoln, London.

Moore, Alan (2011) *No Straight Lines, Making Sense of our Non-linear World*, Bloodstone Books, Cambridge.

Naydler, Jeremy (2009) *The Future of the Ancient World, Essays on the History of Consciousness*, Inner Traditions, Rochester.

Nesfield-Cookson, Bernard (1994) *Rudolf Steiner's Vision of Love*, Sophia Books, London.

O'Donohue, John (1997) *Anam Cara, Spiritual Wisdom from the Celtic World*, Transworld Ireland, London.

Omond, Tasmin (2014) 'Nothing Short of a Consumer Revolution Will Change the World', *Resurgence,* Issue 283.

Osbourne, Roger (2006) *Civilization, A New History of the Western World*, Jonathan Cape, London.

Overy, Richard (2006) *The Times: Complete History of the World*, Times Books, London.

Parsons, Tony (1995) *The Open Secret,* Open Secret Publishing, Cranbourne.

Pascale, Richard *et al.* (2010) *The Power of Positive Deviance, How Unlikely Innovators Solve the World's Toughest Problems,* Harvard Business Press, Boston.

Pert, Candace (1998) *Molecules of Emotion*, Simon and Schuster Ltd., London.

Platon, Nicolas (1966) *Crete*, Nagel Publishers, Geneva.

Quinn, Daniel (1995) *Ishmael, An Adventure of the Mind and Spirit*, Bantam/ Turner, New York.

Radden, Jennifer (ed.) (2000) *The Nature of Melancholy, from Aristotle to Kristeva*, Oxford University Press, Oxford.

Rawbotham, Michael (1998) *The Grip of Death, A Study of Modern Money, Debt Slavery and Destructive Economics*, Jon Carpenter, Charbury.

Rayner, Alan (2011) *NaturesScope*, O Books, Winchester.

— (2013) *The Fluid Boundary Logic of Fungi*, Common Knowledge 19:2 Duke University Press, Durham NC.

— (2013) *Inclusional Sustainability, A Natural Way of Life*, p.6 http:// www.bestthinking.com/articles/science/biology_and_nature/ecology/inclusional-sustainability?tab=article

Reynolds, Fiona (2014) 'Seeing Nature', *Resurgence*, Issue 284.

Robinson, Simon & Maria Moraes Robinson (2014*) Holonomics: Business Where People and Planet Matter*, Floris Books, Edinburgh.

Romanyshyn, Robert (2002) *Ways of the Heart, Essays Towards an Imaginal Psychology*, Trivium Publications, Pittsburgh.

Samanta-Laughton, Manjir (2006) *Punk Science, Inside The Mind of God*, O Books, Winchester.

Sardello, Robert (2006) *Silence, The Mystery of Wholeness,* North Atlantic Books, Berkeley.

Saunders, Thomas (2007) *The Authentic Tarot, Discovering Your Inner Self,* Watkins, London.

Scharmer, Otto & Katrin Kaufer (2013) *Leading From The Emerging Future, From Ego-System To Eco-System Economies,* Berret-Koehler Publishers, San Francisco.

Schumacher, E.F (1973) *Small is Beautiful, A Study of Economics as if People Mattered,* Penguin Group, London

Senge, Peter *et al.* (2004) *Presence, Human Purpose and the Field of the Future*, SoL, Cambridge MA.

Sennett, Richard (2008) *The Craftsman*, Penguin Books, London

Shakespeare, William (1606) *King Lear, Act 1 Scene 2* http://www.shake-speare-monologues.org/plays/32?expand=1.

Sheldrake, Rupert (1990) *The Rebirth of Nature, The Greening of Science and God*, Park Street Press, Rochester Vermont.

— (2012) *The Science Delusion, Freeing The Spirit of Enquiry*, Coronet, London.

Shepard, Paul (1996) *The Others, How Animals Made Us Human*, Island, Washington.

Shiva, Vandana (2014) 'Seed Freedom', *Resurgence*, Issue 278.

Skrbina, David (2007) *Panpsychism in the West*, MIT Press, Cambridge MA.

Small, Meredith (1999) *Our Babies, Ourselves, How Biology and Culture Shape the Way We Parent*, Anchor Books, New York.

Smith, Cyprian (2004) *The Way of Paradox, Spiritual Life As Taught By Meister Eckhart*, Darton Longman and Todd, London.

Soromenho-Marques, Viriato (2012) 'The Art of Living', *Resurgence*, Issue 272.

Speth, James Gustave (2008) *The Bridge at the Edge of the World, Capitalism, the Environment, and Crossing from Crisis to Sustainability*, Yale University Press, New Haven.

Stamets, Paul (2005) *Mycelium Running, How Mushrooms Can Help Save the World*, Ten Speed Press, Berkeley.

Stevens, Anthony (1994) *Jung, A Very Short Introduction*, Oxford University Press, Oxford.

Strauss, Leo (1989) *An Introduction to Political Philosophy: Ten Essays, The Three Waves of Modernity*, Eds. by Halail Gildin, Wayne State University Press, Detroit.

Sumedho, Ajahn (2004) *Intuitive Awareness*, Amaravati Publications, Herts.

Swimme, Brian (1999) *The Hidden Heart of The Cosmos, Humanity and the New Story*, Orbis Books, New York.

Tarnas, Richard (2010) *The Passion of the Western Mind, Understanding the Ideas That Have Shaped Our World View*, Pimlico, London.

Taylor, Steve (2005) *The Fall, The Insanity of the Ego in Human History and The Dawning of A New Era*, O Books, Winchester.

Teilhard de Chardin, Pierre (1977) *Hymn of the Universe*, William Collins, Fount Paperbacks, London.

Temenos Academy Review (2013) Number 16, The Temenos Academy, Ashford.

Temenos (1992) Number 13, The Temenos Academy, Ashford.

Thoreau, Henry David (1862) *Walking Part II*, cited http://thoreau.eserver.org/walking2.html.

Tolle, Eckhart (1999) *The Power of Now, A Guide To Spiritual Enlightenment*, Hodder & Stoughton, London.

— (2005) *A New Earth, Awakening to your Life's Purpose*, Penguin, London.

Totton, Nick (2011) *Wild Therapy, Undomesticating Inner and Outer worlds*, PCCS Books, Ross-on-Wye.

Van Lysebeth, André (1995) *Tantra, The Cult of the Feminine*, Weiser Books, San Francisco.

Watson, Lyall (1974) *SuperNature, A Natural History of the Supernatural*, Coronet, Aylesbury.

— (1986) *Earthworks, Ideas on the Edge of Natural History*. Hodder and Stoughton, Sevenoaks.

Watts, Michael (2011) *The Philosophy of Heidegger*, Acumen, Durham.

Wilber, Ken (1981) *Up From Eden*, Quest Books, Wheaton.

— (2001) *A Theory of Everything, An Integral Vision for Business, Politics, Science and Spirituality*, Gateway, Dublin.

Wilhelm, Richard & Carl Jung (1972) *The Secret of the Golden Flower, A Chinese Book of Life*, Routledge & Kegan Paul, London.

Wilson, Colin (1985) *A Criminal History of Mankind*, Grafton, London.

Williams, Rowan (2014) 'What the Body Knows', *Resurgence*, Issue 283.

Zimmerman, Mary Jane (2004) *Being Nature's Mind: Indigenous Ways of Knowing and Planetary Consciousness* http://www.delvingdeeper.org/pdfs/being.pdf.

Index

Abram, David 43, 108, 130, 145, 152

abstract rationality *see* rationalism

active imagination 118

active seeing 108, 116

active transport 76

Age of Enlightenment 31

Akasha 91, 126, 145, 151

alpha thinking 63f

Anderson, Ray 12

animal communication 83

anima mundi see World Soul

animism 55f, 84f

anthroposophy *see* Steiner, Rudolf

anti-matter 94

Aquinas, Thomas 51

Aristotle 23, 45f, 52f, 64

artisan 160

attunement 128f, 142f, 165–73

Aurobindo, Sri 105

authenticity 19, 110, 117, 124, 138, 167, 170

Avens, Roberts 95

Bachelard, Gaston 125

Backster, Cleve 83

bacteria 79f

Barfield, Owen 63–66

Baring, Anne 54, 59

Bateson, Gregory 11, 27f, 75, 131, 159

Berman, Morris 32

Bernays, Edward 16f

Berry, Thomas 102

beta thinking 63f

bifurication 26

biodiversity 12, 29

black hole principle 92

Blake, William 120, 168

bodymind 123, 169

Bohm, David 90, 100, 136

Bond, Pippa 164

Bourgeault, Cynthia 116, 147

brain
— hemispheres 36, 43, 67f
— wave patterns 82

Brand, William 82

Breytenbach, Anna 83

Broglie, Louis de 89

Bruno, Giordiano 51

Buddha 112

Buddhism 104, 112

Buhner, Stephen Harrod 123, 148

Campanella, Tommaso 51f

Campbell, Joseph 50

capitalism 17f, 161

Cartesian science *see* Descartes

Cashford, Jules 54, 59, 61, 62

Chardin, Teilhard de 99f

Charles, HRH The Prince of Wales 30

Childre, Doc 162
— *HeartMath* 162

Chin, Nan Huai 138

Choy, Peter Chin Kean 115

Christ *see* Jesus Christ

Christ consciousness 100

Christian theology 47–51

Cicero, Marcus Tullius 42

Cleese, John 163

Coleridge, Samuel Taylor 118

communion 144f

competitive exclusion 24

Confucius 109

consciousness 14, 86, 92, 95–97, 102

consumer 17, 160f

consumerism 16–22
Corbin, Henry 117f, 124, 173
cosmic rhythm 130f
Council 163f
Crawford, Matthew 160
creativity 160, 163f
Crouch, Colin 20
Curtis, Adam 18

Dao Lee, Tsung 94
dark energy 90, 94
Darwin, Charles 24–28, 26, 66, 75
Dawkins, Richard 26f
death 81, 114, 136f, 154
debt mountain 20f
Debussy's, Claude 126
deep ecology 102
Democritus 39f
de-sacralisation 32, 53, 95, 130, 157
Descartes, René 31f, 34, 52
Diamond, Stanley 129
Dillard, Annie 119, 140
dinergy 142f, 152, 164
Dirac, Paul 90
diversity 78, 142f see also biodiversity
Doczi, György 142
dominator model 59–62, 79, 131
Drucker, Peter 158
dualism 32, 35, 37, 76, 95, 155

Eckhart, Meister 117
ecological philosophy 101f
ecological succession 78
ecological thinking 165–67
ecology 23, 165f see also deep ecology,
    facilitation ecology
ecology of mind 28
ecopsychology 110
education 160, 166
ego-consciousness 71–73, 85, 101,
    113, 117–20, 124f, 145
ego explosion 58, 62–64, 71f
egotism 20, 111, 143, 158
Einstein, Albert 35, 63, 87
Eisenstein, Charles 161, 163
Eisler, Riane 59, 61

electromagnetic (EM) field 77, 87, 122
Emerson, Ralph Waldo 43
empathic resonance 125f
empiricism 31, 34, 65, 107
envy 172
Eriugena, Johannes Scotus 50
Euclid 46, 69, 148f
evolution 23–30, 81, 154–56
excessive competition 28f

facilitation ecology 81
Feild, Reshad 142, 171
final participation 63f
Fisher, Andy 22, 110
Foreman, Jon 16
Freud, Sigmund 16

Gadamer, Hans-Georg 107
Gassendi, Pierre 32
Gendlin, Eugene 115
genetic mutation 25
Gilbert, Jeremy 164
gnosticism 49, 107, 118
God 48, 62, 65, 173
goddess 60f, 137, 145
Goethe, Johann von 67, 101, 106,
    108, 166
Goodwin, Brian 26
Great Mother see goddess
greed 16, 18, 22
Griffin, David Ray 98
Griffiths, Jay 132
Grof, Stanislaf 86

Haisch, Bernard 88, 151
Hamilton, Robert 19f
Hanh, Thich Nhat 171
Harding, Stephan 57, 80, 101
harmony 142f
Hartshorne, Charles 98
Harvey, Graham 55
heart 121–23, 145–47, 161f
Heidegger, Martin 105f, 108, 110
Heraclitus 124
Herder, Johann 42
Hobbes, Thomas 16, 31, 33

holism 154
Holland, Jack 49
holomovement 90, 100
holonomic thinking 166
humility 138f, 146, 166, 172
Husserl, Edmund 106

imaginal realm 117f, 173
imagination 118, 120
Implicate and Explicate Order 100
indigenous people 28, 48, 60, 121,
        127f, 134
individualism 16, 20, 128, 159
individuation 112f, 115, 119, 129,
        159, 168
intentionality 106
Islamic theology 47, 62

James, William 96f
Jesus Christ 48f, 51, 65, 100, 112,
        117 see also Christian theology
Judaism 62, 65, 86, 145
Jung, Carl 83, 112f, 134, 145

Kaku, Michio 90
Kali 137
Kaufer, Katrin 163
Keller, Catherine 99, 104, 133
kenosis 116
Kerr, Margaret 113
Key, David 113
Khosa, K. 169
King, Ursula 99
Kingsley, Peter 40
Kline, Nancy 162
Kojeve, Alexandre 160
Kovel, Joel 20
Kuhn, Thomas 135
Kumar, Satish 102

Lagarde, Christine 12
Lakota 127
Lao-Tzu 104, 142
Laszlo, Ervin 91
Lawrence, D.H. 55
leadership 138f

Le Bon, Gustave 16
Lebow, Victor 17
Lee, Tsung Dao 94
Lewis, C.S. 23
Lipton, Bruce 76
love 161f, 170–73
Lovins, Hunter 143
Lushwala, Arkan 127, 131, 145

Macartney, Tim 137
Magueijo, Joao 92
Margulis, Lynn 75
Maudsley, Henry 31
Maxwell, James Clerk 87
Maxwell, Rashid 117
May, Gerald 123
McCraty, Rollin 122
McGilchrist, Iain 36, 43, 46, 58, 63,
        67, 129, 163
meditation 115f, 123f, 173
membrane 47f
Merleau-Ponty, Maurice 107f, 111
metamorphosis 146f
Milne, Joseph 11, 45
mind see consciousness
mind focus 82
Minoan culture 60
modern consciousness 65
modernity 52f
monism 76, 104, 155
monoculture 78
Moore, Alan 162
Moore, C.J. 12
morphic resonance 84f
Mother Teresa 162
mundus imaginalis see imaginal realm
mycelia 80f

Naess, Arne 102
Nagarjuna 104
natural inclusion 148–57
natural selection see evolution
nature 32f, 53, 77–86, 95f, 98, 100,
        102, 107, 109–11, 113, 124,
        127, 149, 164–68
— Nature of Business, The 165

Naydler, Jeremy 53
Neo-Darwinism 23, 26, 35, 66, 155, 157
Neolithic
— art 61
— revolution 57
Neo-Platonism 31–33, 47, 50
neural cells 121
new animism 84f
Newton's Laws of Motion 52
Nig Yong, Cheng 94
non-local
— consciousness 86
— quantum 89f
— sensing 82–84

objectification 33–35, 52f, 65f, 95, 106f
O'Donohue, John 148
omega point 100
original participation 63f
Orpheus 39f, 51

paganism 31, 33, 50, 65
panpsychism 102
panentheism 104, 152
pantheism 103
paradigm shift 135, 158, 167f
Parmenides 39f
Parsons, Tony 109
participatory
— evolution 105
— consciousness 101
patriarchy 58f, 65
perception horizon 92
permeability 76f, 105, 114, 128, 130, 146, 149, 155, 165f, 169
Pert, Candace 123
phenomenology 106f, 166, 169
Planck, Max 87, 89
Plato 43f, 47, 64, 70
Plotinus 47
presencing 108f, 123, 166, 169
Pre-socratics 39, 46
process philosophy 98
process theology 98
public relations 16, 18, 20

punctuated evolution 25
pure attention 115
Puritanism 52
Pythagoras 39, 44, 60, 112

quantum theory 91f, 148, 151, 153
quantum vacuum 87f, 91, 151
Quincey, Christian de 77, 97, 105
Quinn, Daniel 29
quorum sensing 80

radical democracy 164
random variation 25
rationalism 34f, 41, 53, 66, 99
Rawbothan, Michael 22
Rayner, Alan 148, 151, 155–57
reason 40–42, 47, 52, 97
rebirth 51, 135, 137
reciprocity 78, 108, 111, 130, 142f, 145, 156f, 168
Reformation 31, 52, 70
regenesis 165
Renaissance 51f
renewal 134f
resentment 172
reverie 125
Reynolds, Fiona 167
Robinson, Maria Moraes & Simon 166
Romanyshyn, Robert 125
Roosevelt, Franklin D. 17
Rumi, Jalal ad-Din Muhammad 171
Russell, Bertrand 135

sacred feminine 60f, 144f
sacred masculine 144f
Sagan, Dorion 75
Samata-Laughton, Manjir 90, 92
Sanders-Sardello, Cheryl 108
Sardello, Robert 125f
Scharmer, Otto 138, 163
Schlitz, Marilyn 82
Schumacher, E.F. 160
scientific positivism 31f
scientific revolution 31, 65f, 73
self-actualisation 18
self-realisation 112f, 145

Sennett, Richard 160
shamanism 45, 51, 53, 55f, 107, 111,
    114, 124, 127, 144
Shakespeare, William 75
Shakti 144, 151
Shekinah 62, 145
Sheldrake, Rupert 58, 84f
Shiva, Vandana 30, 144
Simard, Suzanne 81
Skolimowski, Henryk 101
Skrbina, David 103
Small, Meredith 128
Smith, Cyprian 173
social Darwinism 24
Socrates 39f
soil 79
Sophia 38, 160
soul 124f
Spencer, Herbert 24
Speth, Joseph Gustav 135
spiral 93, 113f, 151
Stamets, Paul 80
St Augustine 49
Steiner, Rudolf 67, 101, 161
Stevens, Anthony 113
St Francis of Assisi 50
Stoic philosophy 41
Strauss, Leo 52
string theory 89f
Sufism 104, 117, 153
survival of the fittest *see* Darwin
Swimme, Brian 91

Tao 99, 104, 126, 145, 147, 153
Tantra 144
Tarnas, Richard 45
Taylor, Steve 56, 58, 63, 71–73, 131

telepathy 82, 85, 90
Thales 39f, 103, 173
Thoreau, Henry David 38, 131
togetherness 128
Tolle, Eckhart 108
torus field 122
Totton, Nick 132
triskele 113f
truth 99

urbanisation 54, 62

Van Lysebeth, André 144
vanity 172
variable speed of light 91

Watson, Lyall 84
wave-particle duality 89
Weinberg, Steven 87
Wheeler, John Archibald 101
Whitehead, Alfred North 97f
Wilber, Ken 45, 58
wildness 131f
Williams, Rowan 168
Wilson, Colin 68
witchcraft 144
Wordsworth, William 77
World Soul 31f, 45, 47, 51, 53, 66,
    109, 113, 126, 146
written word 42f

Yahweh 62, 65
yin and yang 143, 151
Yong, Cheng Nig 94

Zimmerman, Mary Jane 131

About the Author

Giles Hutchins applies twenty years business experience to the emergence of a new paradigm. Formerly a management consultant for KPMG, more recently Global Sustainability Director for Atos International, co-founder of BCI: Biomimicry for Creative Innovation, ambassador for Embercombe, advisor for Akasha Innovation, he speaks and writes about the transformation to new ways of operating, inspired by and in harmony with nature. His first book, *The Nature of Business*, received much praise on both sides of the Atlantic.

Giles blogs at www.thenatureofbusiness.org and tweets @gileshutchins

More praise for *The Illusion of Separation*

Stephan Harding, Head of Holistic Science, Schumacher College

'In this wonderful book, Giles Hutchins helps us to understand the cultural roots of the current crisis and suggests modes of leadership that can help us to find a more fruitful relationship with nature. Well written, well researched and full of insight, this book will open your heart and mind to a deeper way of being in the world.'

Mary Midgley, philosopher, author of *Are You an Illusion*?

'This is a well-expressed book on a fearfully important topic. Read it!'

Ian Skelly, broadcaster and writer, co-author of *Harmony* by HRH The Prince of Wales

'As the world cries out for the shift in perception we know is needed, this is a positive response to the deep seated crisis we face. We may be aware of being, but we have lost contact with the 'beingness' of which we are aware. But how do we "opt in" rather than opt out? How do we 'participate' in creation, rather than seek its control and mere consumption? Here lie the answers. Ours is not the generation to enjoy the fruits of such a shift. As this book so ably demonstrates, it is our task is to make the turning possible. The brilliance of it is that it explains how.'

Simon Robinson, author of *Holonomics*

'*The Illusion of Separation* is a richly thought-provoking journey which teaches us how we can rediscover our humanity, and become inspirational leaders and authentic co-creators.'

Tim 'Mac' Macartney, Founder of Embercombe and author of *Finding Earth, Finding Soul*

'Giles Hutchins's new book *The Illusion of Separation* took me on a roller-coaster journey of ideas, distant memories, broken dreams, and new horizons. He has spread a map at our feet and dares us to look. We, the prodigal species, who with Prometheus' help, stole fire from the gods and imagined ourselves superior. And where does he leave us? Giles is on a personal journey walking home and the path is wide with room for me and you, and all our friends. Home to our true place of belonging.'

Peter Hawkins, author and Professor of Leadership, Henley Business School

'The biggest challenge facing our world today is the urgent need for the human species to evolve its collective ways of thinking. Not since reading the work of Fritjof Capra, have I read a book that so clearly brings together many of the ideas, research and writing that provide the ingredients to help us explore the transformation in our ways of seeing, thinking and being. *The Illusion of Separation* is medicine we all need.'

You may also be interested in...

Holonomics

Business Where People and Planet Matter

Simon Robinson &
Maria Moraes Robinson

'*A powerful antidote to today's dominant culture*'
– Fritjof Capra

Businesses around the world are facing rapidly changing economic and social situations. Business leaders and managers must be ready to respond and adapt in new, innovative ways.

The authors of this groundbreaking book argue that people in business must adopt a 'holonomic' way of thinking, a dynamic and authentic understanding of the relationships within a business system, and an appreciation of the whole. Complexity and chaos are not to be feared, but rather are the foundation of successful business structures and economics.

Holonomics presents a new world view where economics and ecology are in harmony. Using real-world case studies and practical exercises, the authors guide the reader in a new, holistic approach to business, towards a more sustainable future where both people and planet matter.

 Also available as an eBook

florisbooks.co.uk

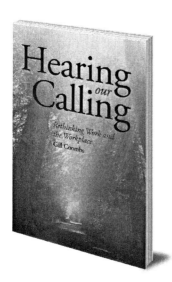

Hearing our Calling

Rethinking Work and the Workplace

Gill Coombs

For many of us, work is a source of anxiety rather than joy, and our workplace routine has become a strain on our lives. This unique book explores whether it's possible to develop a world of work which is, in fact, joyful, fulfilling and good for our health.

Insightful and practical, *Hearing our Calling* traces the history of work, challenging current work practices and routines we take for granted. Drawing on her extensive work with different organisations, the author exposes the corporate world and reveals a surprising and beautiful alternative. She argues that we all have a 'calling', and that hearing it is especially important in times of widespread unemployment and economic hardship.

This lucid and readable book invites us to think differently about how and where we work, both individually and as a society, and offers the potential for real change.

 Also available as an eBook

florisbooks.co.uk

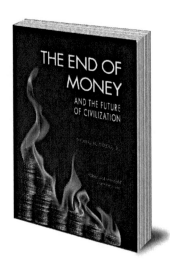

The End of Money and the Future of Civilisation

Thomas H. Greco

'*A refreshing read into the ails of the current global financial system*'
– The Ecologist

Like the proverbial fish that doesn't know what water is, we swim in an economy built on money that few of us comprehend. And what we don't know is hurting us. *The End of Money and the Future of Civilization* demystifies the subjects of money, banking and finance by tracing historical landmarks and important evolutionary shifts that have changed the essential nature of money. Greco's masterful work lays out the problems and then looks to the future for the next stage in money's evolution that can liberate us from the current grip of centralized and politicized money power.

Greco provides specific design proposals and exchange-system architectures for local, regional, national, and global financial systems. He offers innovative strategies for their implementation and outlines actions that grassroots organizations, businesses, and governments will need to take to achieve success.

Associative Economics

Spiritual Activity for the Common Good

Gary Lamb

Associative economics is a philosophy of money developed from the ideas of Rudolf Steiner. It places human beings at the centre of all economic activity, replacing the power of unseen 'market forces' with personal freedom and responsibility.

In this comprehensive book, Gary Lamb explains associative economics, its background and principles, and its potential to change our world, along with possible pitfalls. He gives examples of successful projects and offers practical small steps that we can make to improve our situation.

This is a useful introduction to an important form of alternative economics.

Published by AWSNA.
Available from Floris Books.

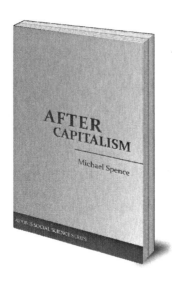

After Capitalism

Michael Spence

Around the world, people are increasingly waking up to the seriousness of our social, environmental and economic situation, and the realisation that the thinking that has brought us here is utterly insufficient for taking us forward in a humane, holistic and healthy way.

This book offers an accessible yet radically unconventional perspective on our current crises. It helps the reader understand how human society, especially the economy, works, and how our inherited social structures have contributed to the growing gap between rich and poor.

Drawing inspiration from Rudolf Steiner's insights, but not based on any one economic, political or religious belief system, Michael Spence shows how society consists of an interweaving of three different sectors, and how a fresh understanding of them can help us work towards a better world.

Published by Adonis Press.
Available from Floris Books.